FEARLESS AND FLAWLESS PUBLIC SPEAKING

With Power, Polish, and Pizazz

Reach for the stars!

Mary Miller Drummond

MAR 06 1995

FEARLESS AND FLAWLESS PUBLIC SPEAKING

With Power, Polish, and Pizazz

Mary-Ellen Drummond

Pfeiffer
& COMPANY

Amsterdam • Johannesburg • London
San Diego • Sydney • Toronto

Editor: JoAnn Padgett
Assistant Editor: Heidi Callinan
Page Compositor: Nicola Ruskin
Cover: John Odam Design Associates

ISBN:
Trade Paper 0-89384-220-6
Hardcover 0-88390-376-8

Library of Congress Catalog Card Number 92-51017

Printed in the United States of America.
Printing 1 2 3 4 5 6 7 8 9 10

Contents

Acknowledgments

I wish to thank my friends in the National Speakers Association, Toastmasters International, and the American Society for Training and Development for their support and inspiration.

I collaborated with Deborah Fairbanks, a learning specialist, to revise my first edition of this book. I thank her for helping me make this a "learner friendly" guide to developing powerful communication skills.

My special gratitude goes to Ruth Holton, Maureen Rafael, Eva Shaw, Sheryl Roush, Betsy Mill, and my husband, John, for their ideas, suggestions, time, and support.

Introduction

I believe that anyone can conquer fear by doing the things he fears to do, provided he keeps doing them until he gets a record of successful experiences behind him.

Eleanor Roosevelt

A Stanford University study revealed that a person's success in life can be predicted by the way he or she answers this question: Are you willing to get up and give a speech right now? Most people would say, "No way!"

According to the *Book of Lists*, speaking before a group is the number one fear—far ahead of the fear of heights, insects and bugs, financial problems, deep water, illness, and even the fear of death. (Fear of death tied with the fear of illness for the sixth greatest fear.)

Why are we so fearful of speaking? In a recent seminar, more than 1,500 people were polled as to why they did not pursue certain goals or take more risks. The overwhelming response was *fear of failure*. Perhaps we fear that we will look foolish or stupid in front of an audience. Maybe we are self-conscious about the way we will look or come across. We may recall painful, embarrassing moments in our pasts when we were made fun of or criticized for our performances. Whatever the reasons, many of us are held back by our fears. If we overcome our fears of public speaking or communicating before a group, we set ourselves on the path to greater success.

Public-speaking skills and improved communication skills can accelerate a person's self-confidence. I have seen incredible turnarounds in people who were once thought of as timid, shy, unassertive, quiet, and without leadership skills. I was once extremely shy and easily intimidated; but I discovered that when people learn the skills necessary to conquer their fears, all things are possible.

As Sir Edmund Hillary said, "It is not the mountain we conquer, but ourselves." It is true that the greater your fear, the more self-confidence you will gain by facing the challenge of overcoming it. Don't avoid the challenge. Discover and be your personal best. You, too, can communicate with power, polish, and pizazz.

Getting the Most From This Book

Section One of this book deals with essential communication skills. Managing your fears, developing your vocal qualities, establishing meaningful eye contact, using your body effectively, and strengthening your listening skills all build personal confidence and effectiveness. These skills can benefit you in both personal and professional interactions.

Sections Two and Three focus on successfully preparing and presenting your ideas to a group, regardless of size. These chapters build on the essential skills addressed in Section One. You will find some advanced techniques in Section Three for particular speaking occasions, such as formal introductions and handling the media.

Section Four provides ideas and techniques for continually improving the communication process. From every presentation or significant communication exchange, you can extract the learning and apply it to your next speaking opportunity.

Doing what you fear most is the way to conquer your fear. The way to become a more effective speaker and communicator is to practice speaking on an ongoing basis. Every time you speak, whether you're speaking on the phone, at a meeting, during a party, or making a formal presentation, you are practicing the art of public speaking. Being more aware of how you come across to others, objectively evaluating yourself, and working on becoming more effective is the path to improvement. The tips, techniques, and exercises in this book will coach you along the path to better communication performance.

Complete the following three work sheets to determine what type of communicator you are and what you can do to improve your skills.

Work Sheet 1
Describe Yourself

Consider the following list of descriptors. Which ones currently identify you? Which ones have you heard used to describe you? Take a minute to circle those that give a snapshot of how you see yourself right now.

abrupt	cold	dominating
aggressive	complimentary	dull
agreeable	conceited	effervescent
amiable	concerned	egocentric
animated	confident	empathic
anxious	conservative	energetic
articulate	considerate	enthusiastic
assertive	critical	even
attentive	cynical	exhausted
belligerent	decent	fair
calm	decisive	flexible
caring	defensive	frank
charming	deliberate	friendly
cheerful	detailed	frustrated
childlike	dignified	fun
clear	disciplined	funny

fussy	modest	refined
gentle	morose	resentful
generous	mumbler	reserved
good-natured	needy	rude
gracious	negative	sarcastic
grateful	nervous	serious
greedy	nice	short
grim	nuisance	shy
hard working	off-beat	sincere
honest	off-color	soft-spoken
hostile	offensive	subdued
hot-headed	open	superior
humble	organized	sweet
humorous	overbearing	sympathetic
immature	perfectionist	tactful
inferior	persistent	temperamental
intelligent	petty	tenacious
inviting	polite	trusting
jealous	pompous	trustworthy
jovial	positive	truthful
joyful	powerful	vivacious
judgmental	prejudiced	warm
jumpy	pretentious	weak
laborious	professional	wise
lazy	radiant	wishy-washy
leader	radical	witty
mature	rambler	wordy

Work Sheet 2
Communication Profile

	Yes	No	Sometimes
My voice is easily heard, and people rarely ask me to repeat what I've said.		✓	
In groups, I find it easy to speak up to express my ideas and opinions.	✓		
I find that others usually do not interrupt me.	✓		
I am able to deliver a presentation without relying on notes.		✓	
My voice does not fade at the ends of sentences.			✓
My speech delivery and everyday conversation are free of distractions such as uh, um, you know, and so on.		✓	
I use vocal variety and feeling to give my words meaning and emphasis.		✓	
I am comfortable using eye contact to establish bonds with my listeners.		✓	
I am a good listener and do not interrupt.	✓		
I ask good questions and know how to draw others into a conversation.		✓	
I am able to think clearly and quickly when called on to speak in an impromptu situation.		✓	
My gestures, body language, and image are consistent with my message.		✓	
I use proper grammar and build my vocabulary.			✓

	Yes	No	Sometimes
I effectively use visual aids, examples, and anecdotes to reinforce my message.	____	____	____
I am overly critical of others.	____	____	____
I am abrupt with people who are annoying.	____	____	____
I am too tough on myself. I am my own worst critic.	____	____	____
I often praise others publicly.	____	____	____
Others often ask for my opinion and advice.	____	____	____
I welcome the opportunity to speak at a meeting.	____	____	____
I feel comfortable when addressing a large audience.	____	____	____
I find it easy to evaluate others with fairness.	____	____	____
I seek ways to build my speaking abilities and communication skills.	____	____	____

Work Sheet 3
Set Goals

To develop your presentation skills, it is useful to examine your current skills and then determine which areas you need to work on. Clarifying your own interests will help you glean what is most relevant to you.

1. Select five words from the list of descriptors that best describe you.

   _____

   Then select five words that describe how you would like to be perceived.

   _____

   Write a brief paragraph using these words to envision yourself positively.

   _____

   _____

   _____

   _____

   _____

2. Refer to the Communication Profile and list the top three goals that you would like to achieve. For example, if you responded no to "I am comfortable using eye contact," your goal might be to feel comfortable using eye contact.

   _____

   _____

   _____

   _____

   _____

Section One

Essential Communication Skills

This section gives you an opportunity to learn some essential skills that will benefit you in any communication exchange. It focuses on the skills involved in preparing a more formal presentation.

1

Taming Your Fear

I have often been afraid, but I would not give in to it. I simply acted as though I was not afraid, and presently the fear disappeared.
Theodore Roosevelt

At my seminars I ask the audience, "How many of you love to give speeches?" Usually, only a very few will raise their hands. It is more normal to fear speaking than to enjoy it. However, it is possible to learn how to enjoy yourself, or at least make the experience a positive one.

Almost everyone experiences fear of speaking until they learn how to overcome their fear. The remainder of this chapter gives you some techniques to help you act as though you are not afraid. In time, your fear will diminish.

Learning to overcome your fear of speaking is a simple process of channeling your nervous excitement into positive energy. This process involves using some proven techniques: affirming, breathing, and composing yourself—the ABCs of dealing with nervousness. As you use these techniques, you will condition yourself to give a new, more effective response. When you hear, "Will you present your ideas to our group next week?" or "We need you to give a presentation or class on...," your response will be a relaxed but enthusiastic "Certainly. Let's talk about what you'd like."

Creating an optimal state of being with your mind and body is the first skill in effective speaking.

Affirmations

The first thing you should do is change the way you talk to yourself. Rather than saying, "Oh, I'm so nervous" or "I am scared to death," start saying, "I am excited about this speech (talk, performance, or whatever)." Your body and mind cannot differentiate between fear and excitement since the same physiological responses occur with both emotions.

Characteristics of
Affirmative Statements

- Tell yourself what you want, not what you don't want.

- Use positive verbs when you talk to yourself.

- Describe yourself succeeding right now, in the present.

Tell yourself what you want, not what you don't want.

Many speakers will say, "I just know that I'm going to forget my speech." And, sure enough, they do. It's the self-fulfilling prophecy at work. You can choose positive or negative self-expectancy. Why not choose the positive? Expect the best, and you'll be amazed at how often you get the results you want. Telling yourself what you want to feel is far more positive than reinforcing negative feelings and fears.

Use positive verbs when you talk to yourself.

Listen to yourself when you are dreading or are unsure of presenting your ideas. You might hear, "I can't do this," " It'll never work," "I don't have the experience, knowledge, looks..." When you use positive verbs, you will feel more in control. Say, "I *can* do this," "I *deserve* to succeed," "I *choose* to make it work." This creates a proactive perspective, which directs your energy toward a positive outcome.

Describe yourself succeeding right now, in the present.

The human brain is similar to a computer in some ways. Much like we can program a computer, we can program our thoughts about speaking. Positive, effective speakers [actors, athletes, leaders, and so forth] presume their success. They have learned to think and see their success in the present moment. You can direct your own thoughts by declaring, "I welcome this opportunity to share and clarify my ideas. I am prepared and calm. I see myself communicating effectively and enjoying it!"

As you learn to talk to yourself with positive words in terms of what you want, you will harness an inner power to propel your presentations. You might notice a boost in other areas of your life as well.

Examples of Affirmative Self-Talk

I am going to do well today.
I will remember my presentation.
The audience wants to hear what I have to say.
I am enthusiastic when presenting my ideas.
I see myself presenting with power and pizazz.

I am calm and relaxed.
I am excited about this presentation.
With each breath I take, I feel calmer and more assured.
I think only of the positive outcomes I seek.
I can do this. I want to do well and enjoy the process.

When I think of speaking to this group, I smile with confidence.
I remember to relax my muscles and breathe deeply as I rehearse, prepare, and approach my audience.
I open my talk with humor to help myself and the audience relax and enjoy the information.

I prepare for each presentation.
I organize my thoughts clearly and logically.
I practice my speech, looking for ways to improve it.
I enjoy doing my best.
I dress appropriately and comfortably for the purpose of my talk.

I project myself with power, and I develop my vocal skills.
I stand proudly before my group, balanced and firmly on both feet.
I move deliberately, using my body to reinforce my message.

I don't mind making mistakes as I learn to speak more effectively.
I learn from my errors and become more polished and professional.
I accept feedback from others with poise and openness. I evaluate myself after each presentation, determining which areas need improvement.
I use all opportunities to continue learning and developing my skills.

I communicate with power, polish, and pizazz.

Source: Deborah Fairbanks, a certified Self-Talk Trainer

Try It Now

The following exercise provides an opportunity to begin developing this powerful affirmation technique. Like any new technique, the sooner you use it, the more it becomes integrated in your memory. More important, it is essential to practice this new skill in order to form a more effective automatic response when you are invited to communicate your ideas.

Practice creating affirmative statements, using words you are comfortable saying to yourself. You might select an upcoming event in which you will speak. As you write phrases in your own words, link them to the event. Refer to the Characteristics of Affirmative Statements on page 12.

 As you practice writing affirmations, you will begin to etch new patterns of thought. Write a couple of phrases on a note card and refer to it for several days to develop an *automatic* response.

Breathing

When people get nervous, they often forget to breathe. That may sound silly, but it's true. When we get scared, we sometimes hold our breath; or we begin to breathe with small, shallow breaths from the top of our lungs rather than taking deep breaths from the lower lungs to get the amount of air we need.

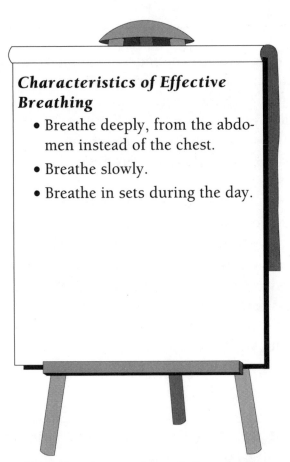

Characteristics of Effective Breathing

- Breathe deeply, from the abdomen instead of the chest.
- Breathe slowly.
- Breathe in sets during the day.

Breathe deeply, from the abdomen instead of the chest.

Place your hand flat on your abdomen with your little finger at the waistline and your thumb resting between the place where your ribs separate. Now take a deep breath. Did you feel your abdomen expand? If yes, then you are breathing correctly. *Abdominal breathing* not only helps to relieve tension, but it also helps you project your voice as well.

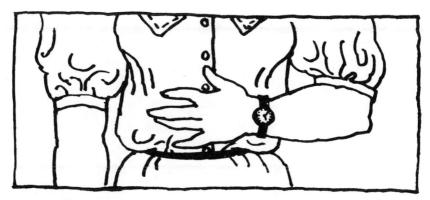

Breathe slowly.

We often breathe faster when we're nervous. Faster breathing requires more breaths to get enough oxygen, making our heart work harder. Slower, deeper breathing provides more oxygen and helps us relax.

Breathe in sets during the day.

If you are in the habit of breathing from the chest and reacting to stress with quicker breaths, you'll want to develop a new habit of slower, abdominal breathing. Try the following exercise to practice breathing, which will boost your speaking confidence and voice.

Try It Now

The following exercise will help you "take five" anytime.

1. Inhale slowly into your abdomen to the count of five. Hold for two counts. Exhale, slowly counting to five.
2. Repeat.
3. Inhale again to the count of five. Hold for two counts. Exhale, slowly counting to five.
4. Repeat.
5. Inhale again to the count of five. Hold for two counts. Exhale, slowly counting to five.

As breathing deeply and slowly five times becomes more comfortable, increase it to ten times. Some people get dizzy at first if they're unaccustomed to deep breathing, so build up to it slowly.

As soon as you agree to speak, begin using this technique to prepare yourself in a calm, confident manner. Also use it prior to speaking to create a physically relaxed state.

 On the back of your affirmation card, write a reminder to take five breaths at least two or three times a day. Refer to your card daily.

Composing Yourself

The third technique for overcoming speaking fears has to do with physically composing yourself. These tips work with your self-talk affirmations and deep breathing to create a mental and physical state that prepares you for speaking with personal power.

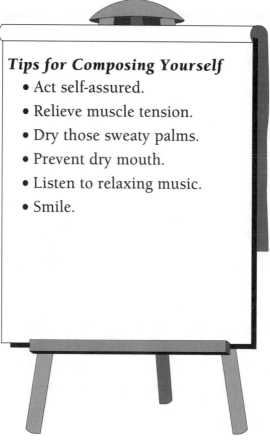

Tips for Composing Yourself
- Act self-assured.
- Relieve muscle tension.
- Dry those sweaty palms.
- Prevent dry mouth.
- Listen to relaxing music.
- Smile.

Act self-assured.

Many times I've been asked, "What should I do when my face turns red or my neck gets blotchy?" Feeling self-conscious about standing in front of an audience may cause this common physical reaction. Here are some tips to help you cope with it.

In advance, visualize yourself looking self-assured as a presenter, with a natural, vibrant complexion.

Focus on the needs of your audience, not on your red face and neck. By concentrating on others, you will take the focus off yourself.

Concentrate on your extremities. For example, use the exercise described for relieving muscle tension to refocus your attention away from your face and neck.

Ask the audience a question, or involve them in the program so that attention is momentarily diverted from you.

Relieve muscle tension.

If you're nervous or unsure of your speaking ability, you may unconsciously develop muscle tension. Use the following exercise whenever you anticipate a speaking situation and find yourself getting tense. It is also beneficial when you are waiting for your turn to speak. People will not be aware of what you are doing if you simply strike a normal pose at the table where you are seated. It has worked wonders for countless speakers.

Pinch your index and middle fingertips against your thumbs. Hold your fingers together in this pinched manner for at least thirty seconds or until your fingers hurt. Then release the pressure. Now experience how relaxed your hands and arms feel. The muscles are forced to relax, which makes you feel more relaxed, too.

You can do this same exercise with your toes. Pretend you're trying to grasp the floor with your toes (through your shoes). Tensing the muscles and holding the position for more than thirty seconds will relax your feet and legs so that they are unlikely to shake.

Stretching is another great relaxer. Before your meeting is called to order, find a restroom and do some stretching exercises. According to trainer Robert Pike, "Most people can reach two inches higher than they think they can." Try reaching that high. Alternate stretching your hands and arms upward, at least ten times. You'll immediately notice the tension reduction.

Dry those sweaty palms.

Many people are concerned about having sweaty palms before and during a presentation or tension-filled situation such as an interview or an important meeting. Sweaty palms can cause you to have increased anxiety about shaking hands with another person. Try rubbing an antiperspirant on your palms (not a deodorant). Experiment with this before the day of your performance to make sure that the antiperspirant you use does not make your hands feel too dry or sticky. You may also want to keep a handkerchief or a tissue tucked in your pocket to help keep your hands dry and perspiration free.

Prevent dry mouth.

Dry mouth is another symptom of fear and nervousness. You may want to have a small mint, a cough drop, or a piece of candy just before you are introduced. Have a glass of water on hand at the lectern. Some speakers rub a small amount of petroleum jelly on their front teeth to prevent their lips from sticking to their teeth during a presentation. Do not chew gum. Avoid taking antihistamines before any presentation because they will make your mouth even drier.

Listen to relaxing music.

Relaxation tapes and slow, soothing music will also help you to ease your nervousness. (Music that has 60 to 70 beats per minute mimics the human heart rate at rest. Look for music by composers such as Pachelbel, Albinoni, Mozart, Handel, and Vivaldi.) Play this type of music while writing, rehearsing, and driving to your presentation.

Smile.

It is very difficult for your brain to register fear when you are smiling. Arnold Glasow said, "Laughter is a tranquilizer with no side effects." A smile can work wonders for you and your audience. Practice smiling as you rehearse. Look at yourself in a mirror or on videotape. Then smile as soon as you begin your presentation. Look as if you are enjoying yourself.

Have you seen speakers who look miserable or simply scared out of their wits? You probably felt fearful for them. Your audience will reflect your mood. Conversely, when you smile, you look more confident and self-assured. The audience feels more at ease and more comfortable, as well. The speaker sets the standard and the mood for the audience.

Thirty minutes or so before you make your presentation, mingle with the group. Smile. Be friendly. Introduce yourself. Learn the names of some of the people you'll be speaking to and some tidbits of information that you may be able to incorporate into your program. During the presentation, focus on the friendly faces in your audience. Talk to people as if you are speaking one-on-one. Focusing on the positive people in your audience and your message for them will take the focus off of yourself, which will make you feel calmer.

Section Two, Preparing to Present, gives additional tips for preparing a positive start.

Before you speak, avoid alcohol, caffeine, and sedatives. Alcohol can blur your mind, slur your speech, and create an unprofessional appearance. Caffeine, found in chocolate, tea, and coffee, is a stimulant and may make you more nervous. Drink plain, uncarbonated beverages. Hot water or herbal tea with a small amount of lemon and honey is better for the voice, throat, and nerves.

Summary

You should probably not completely eliminate a feeling of nervousness before your presentation. Actually you *want* some degree of nervousness. The secret is to enable yourself to *deal* with the nervousness in a positive, constructive way. The techniques and tips in this chapter give you a strategy for redirecting negative fear into positive energy.

Dr. Hans Selye advised that people should learn to "experience stress without distress." Sir Laurence Olivier said that all great performers need some degree of nervous energy to make them great. The best performers are the ones with adrenalin pumping to make them seem energetic, enthusiastic, and excited about their message. Picture a speaker who has no fear, no energy, no enthusiasm, and probably no one awake in the audience either!

Preparation will give you a great deal of comfort. Being prepared and actually delivering a presentation are the biggest confidence builders of all. Sections Two and Three address the topic of preparation and rehearsal so that you will be more at ease.

Before any presentation or important occasion, use the ABCs for empowering yourself.

Affirm yourself looking and being confident, self-assured, and excited. Your subconscious cannot tell if something is imagined or real. Fill your mind with positive thoughts that reinforce your success. See yourself being a winning communicator, and you will be.

Breathe deeply and slowly to nourish yourself with oxygen.

Compose yourself through muscle relaxation and music. Use the tips to dry your palms and wet your mouth. Avoid chemicals that ultimately aggravate your nerves.

Checklist

Use these techniques to develop a new automatic response. Practice them daily, as soon as you are asked to give a presentation, prior to a presentation, and even during the presentation.

Overcoming Fears and Building Personal Power

Affirmative Exercises

- ☐ Tell yourself what you want, not what you don't want.
- ☐ Use positive verbs when you talk to yourself.
- ☐ Describe yourself succeeding right now, in the present.
- ☐ Practice writing affirmations on a note card and refer to it daily.

Breathing Exercises

- ☐ Breathe deeply, from the abdomen instead of the upper chest.
- ☐ Breathe slowly.
- ☐ Breathe in sets during the day. Take five with deep, slow breaths.
- ☐ Carry a reminder to do your deep breathing exercise during the day.

Composure Tips

- ☐ Act self-assured.
- ☐ Relieve muscle tension through your fingers and toes; stretch.
- ☐ Dry those sweaty palms.
- ☐ Prevent dry mouth with candy, petroleum jelly, and water at the lectern.
- ☐ Listen to relaxing music while preparing, rehearsing, and driving to your presentation.
- ☐ Avoid alcohol, caffeine, and sedatives. Drink water or herbal tea.
- ☐ Smile.

2

Polishing Your Voice

A mighty thing is eloquence...nothing so much rules the world.
Pope Pius II

D r. Albert Mehrabian, a professor and researcher at the University of California, Los Angeles, reported that only 7 percent of any message is communicated with words, while 38 percent of the message is relayed by our voice (tone, accent, inflection, pacing, projection, and so on). The way we say something speaks far louder than the actual words. The remaining 55 percent of a message is communicated by nonverbal body language, which is discussed later.

The way we speak conveys a great deal about us. Imagine a person who wants to sound authoritative but has a timid, soft, fading voice. Would you believe this person is an authority on his or her topic? Probably not. Imagine a teacher who doesn't complete sentences and makes many false starts when speaking. Would you believe this person is capable of inspiring students to learn? Probably not. Imagine a person with a loud, booming, aggressive voice. Would you back away from this person? Probably so.

This chapter describes the qualities of a strong, effective voice. Whether you speak face to face or over the telephone, you transmit your message *through* your voice as much as *with* it. Work Sheet 4 provides information about how you see certain communication traits in others. The other exercises in this chapter provide practical tips to help you develop a polished voice. Practicing the vocal qualities you want to employ and putting vitality into your words will heighten your confidence and attractiveness as a speaker.

Work Sheet 4
Assess Your Voice

Examine your opinion on the following questions. Check whether these communication traits annoy to you or not.

	Annoys Me	Doesn't Annoy Me
Interrupting while others are talking	☐	☐
Swearing or using curse words	☐	☐
Mumbling or talking too softly	☐	☐
Talking too loudly	☐	☐
Monotonous, boring voice	☐	☐
Using filler words such as *and um, like um,* and *you know*	☐	☐
A nasal whine	☐	☐
Talking too fast	☐	☐
Poor grammar or mispronouncing words	☐	☐
A high-pitched voice	☐	☐
A foreign accent or a regional dialect	☐	☐

The following provides a summary of a national poll on these same traits.

A Gallup Poll communication survey reported many of the traits that the American people find annoying or not annoying. Here are the results:

	Annoys Me	Doesn't Annoy Me
Interrupting while others are talking	88%	11%
Swearing or using curse words	84%	15%
Mumbling or talking too softly	80%	20%
Talking too loudly	73%	26%
Monotonous, boring voice	73%	26%
Using filler words such as *and um, like um,* and *you know*	69%	29%
A nasal whine	67%	29%
Talking too fast	66%	34%
Poor grammar or mispronouncing words	63%	36%
A high-pitched voice	61%	37%
A foreign accent or a regional dialect	24%	75%

Develop Your Vocal Skills

Based on the results of the Gallup survey, the following skills have been identified for you to practice so that you can become a better communicator.

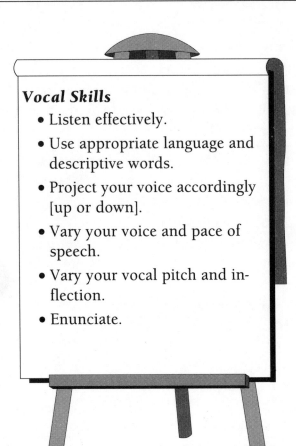

Vocal Skills

- Listen effectively.
- Use appropriate language and descriptive words.
- Project your voice accordingly [up or down].
- Vary your voice and pace of speech.
- Vary your vocal pitch and inflection.
- Enunciate.

Listen effectively.

The most annoying trait listed in the Gallup Poll was interrupting while others are talking. If people interrupt you, try holding up an index finger, or your hand, to signal "Stop. I'm not finished yet." If you tend to interrupt, try letting the other person finish before you interject. Impatient people want to finish the sentence of a person who speaks at a slower pace. Try to encourage the other person without acting impatient. Simply nod, say "I see," or offer other positive listening words.

Being a good listener does not just mean waiting until it is your turn to speak. It involves specific skills. You will find some tips on developing effective listening skills in the next chapter.

Use appropriate language and descriptive words.

Avoid using any objectionable or inappropriate words that may offend even one person in your audience.

The second most annoying trait listed was swearing or using curse words. Many of today's motion pictures have dialogue filled with expletives. When every other word is a swear word, the words become diluted and the audience is desensitized to the impact. These words are unnecessary and a distraction if overused.

Using poor grammar or mispronounced words annoyed 63 percent of people surveyed by the Gallup Poll. If you are not sure of the pronunciation of a word, look it up in the dictionary, ask for help from someone else, or don't use the word in your presentation. Studies have shown that the larger your vocabulary, the higher up the corporate ladder you climb. However, you should not use multisyllabic words when giving a presentation unless the words are necessary. For example, using computer language is appropriate when speaking to a group of computer engineers but inappropriate to a service club.

In general, you should speak at an eighth-grade vocabulary level rather than offend your audience by using words like obfuscate, plethora, or prestidigitation. George Orwell said, "Never use a long word when a short one will do." If you use large, multisyllable words, your audience may think you are pretentious and may be put off by the words. Descriptive word pictures are best. Descriptive words paint the message with color and clarity.

Using filler words such as *and um, like um,* and *you know* annoyed 69 percent of the American people. Ted Kennedy was asked by a national news magazine reporter in the late seventies, "Why do you want to be president of the United States?" His answer filled nearly two-thirds of a page of the news magazine, and he still did not answer the question. Brevity is powerful.

Be certain to use words that are appropriate to the audience and words that will describe your message clearly and creatively.

Project your voice accordingly (up or down).

Mumbling or talking too softly rated third in the most annoying category. Eighty percent of listeners were annoyed by a soft-spoken voice. When people speak too softly, they are conveying that what they have to say isn't important for you to hear. If people often ask you to repeat what you have said, you are probably speaking too softly. Projecting your voice at the appropriate level denotes confidence and a belief in what you are saying.

Breathing from the diaphragm is also essential to good voice projection. Avoid sighing, or releasing your air, before speaking. (Many people do this when they feel tense. Sighing is often a sign of anxiety.) Let the air behind your words project your voice. As a public speaker, you always want to project your voice to the person farthest away from you in the audience. It is annoying not to be able to hear what the speaker is saying.

Projection literally means sending your voice where you want it to go. Most people think that projection means loudness. It simply means making yourself heard. Abraham Lincoln read aloud for at least thirty minutes a day to practice his oratorical skills. When he gave his inaugural address in Washington, D.C., his practice paid off. He spoke to approximately thirty thousand people, without the aid of a microphone, and every word could be heard by the hushed crowd.

You can increase the volume of your voice by training yourself to open your mouth more when you speak. Many times, when we are nervous, we begin to clench our jaws. The tightness inhibits good projection. Voice coaches instruct their students to learn to relax the jaw and thus liberate the voice.

Talking too loudly was rated fourth on the Gallup Poll of most annoying traits. Speaking too loudly is perceived as being very aggressive. Overpowering people by speaking over their words is rude and perceived negatively. Have you ever been at a meeting when you were overrun by someone else? You probably resented the other person's aggression. Have you ever been the person with the loud voice? Notice if people back away from you or shift their weight to their back foot when you are standing and speaking in a group. When seated, a listener might lean back in his or her chair if you are speaking too loudly. This shift in body language is a signal that you need to lower your projection level.

Vary your voice and pace of speech.

A monotonous or boring voice was annoying to 73 percent of the people polled. Think about the times you have been bored by a speaker, teacher, or other person. What was it that bored you? Was it the voice that went on and on without any variation or energy? Recently, I was watching an interview in which one of the panelists said, "Yes, we're really excited about this project." The words, however, were spoken with no excitement—only boredom and lack of enthusiasm. I did not believe that the panelist was excited at all.

Physicians are trained to listen to patients' voices as one way of determining a diagnosis of depression. People who are depressed usually lack vocal vitality. They speak in a monotone and at a slower pace than normal. Your voice reflects what is going on inside of you and in your life.

Talking too fast annoyed 66 percent of the people surveyed (though talking too slow can be just as annoying). The mind can think at an amazingly fast pace, but it is a good idea to vary your pace so that the listener can absorb what you are saying. It can be effective to pause after an important point and perhaps to repeat it so that the importance of the fact is registered. John F. Kennedy was very effective in pacing his words. Think of how he sounded when he said, "Ask not what your country can do for you. Ask what you can do for your country."

Most audiences enjoy listening to a presenter who speaks at a faster pace. According to the Guinness Book of World Records, John F. Kennedy holds the record of speed speaking. In December of 1961, President Kennedy delivered a speech at the rate of 327 words per minute.

The world's fastest talker is Boston's John Moschitta. In 1988, he spoke 545 words in less than a minute. Obviously, more than 500 words per minute only serves to amaze and entertain. Speaking at too fast a pace can also frustrate an audience and make a negative impression.

Speakers often want to rush through their presentations so that they can sit down and get out of the limelight. It takes (and demonstrates) confidence to slow things down a bit and pause occasionally for emphasis. Vary the pace and you will keep your audience more enthralled.

Vary your vocal pitch and inflection.

A high-pitched voice was annoying to 61 percent of the people in the Gallup Poll. American people, in general, seem to prefer a lower pitched voice. Eighty percent of the voice-overs on television and radio are done by men. Higher voices are associated with childlike qualities and are taken less seriously. It is especially important for women to learn to emphasize the lower tones of their voices if they want to come across with more maturity, authority, and credibility. Think about how your voice sounds when you run into someone at a party—someone you haven't seen for a long time and someone whom you're excited to see. Have you ever heard yourself say in a very high-pitched voice, "Oh, I didn't know you'd be here!"?

Learning to drop your pitch takes effort and control. Begin to notice when your voice goes up. Make a conscious effort to bring the level back down. Also, check to see if you are speaking in your natural pitch.

To sound more sure of yourself and of your words, drop your vocal inflection at the ends of statements. Think about how you sound when you ask a question. Does your inflection go up at the end of the question? Many people have this same upward inflection when making statements of fact. If their inflection goes up at the end of the statement, they sound less sure of themselves.

Most people will introduce themselves at a meeting with an upward inflection at the end of each phrase. For example, "My name is Jane Doe (inflection up), I live in San Diego (inflection up), my business is insurance (inflection up)." Imagine Tom Brokaw on the nightly news saying, "Today, the United States raised income taxes." If his inflection went up at the end of the sentence, we would ask ourselves, "Did taxes go up, or didn't they?" Dropping your overall pitch and your inflection at the ends of phrases and sentences will give you the sound of greater power and authority.

Enunciate.

A nasal whine was annoying to 67 percent of the people in the Gallup Poll. Nasality may be lessened by retraining the tongue. When your tongue rises higher than necessary, air is forced to the roof of your mouth and through your nose, giving a more nasal sound to your voice. You will find some exercises for retraining the tongue later in this chapter.

The final element on the Gallup Poll, a foreign accent, annoyed just 24 percent of the people surveyed. Many times, an accent can be an asset. For Americans, the British accent is highly respected and revered. For example, ABC radio's talk show host Michael Jackson, who was born in England, is one of America's most successful and enduring stars of the airwaves. Countless movie stars and recording artists with accents have become box office hits.

In regard to regional accents within the United States, many people are often surprised to learn that one of the most respected regional accents in America is that of Bostonians. Perhaps this respect is due to John F. Kennedy's legacy, or perhaps it is due to so many institutions of higher education that are located in Massachusetts. Many of the most successful professional public speakers come from the southern states. Speakers such as Zig Ziglar, Suzie Humphreys, and Robert Henry seem to have a real knack for storytelling and relating well to an audience.

If you have an accent, learn to use it to your advantage. It may help people remember you. If your accent is something you sincerely don't like and want to lessen or eliminate, contact a voice coach to learn techniques to minimize it.

Tape record yourself and evaluate how you sound. Try to be objective. Ask for feedback from friends, coworkers, and people whose opinions you respect. Decide whether or not your accent is an asset or a liability.

When evaluating your own accent, ask yourself these questions:

- Do you think you are asked about your accent too often?

- Are you annoyed when people ask you, "Where are you from originally?" or "Where were you born?"

- Do you think you are stereotyped because of your accent?

- Does your accent cause you to feel self-conscious?

If you decide that it is important to change the way you sound, be patient. It will take months of modification, taping, and practicing to alter your accent. Just as actors learn to change accents, you can too.

Try It Now

The following activities and tips will help you develop better voice and diction technique. Like any new technique, the sooner you practice it, the greater the chance you'll continue to use and strengthen it. Try the activities that fit your needs and make a commitment with yourself to continue developing those areas.

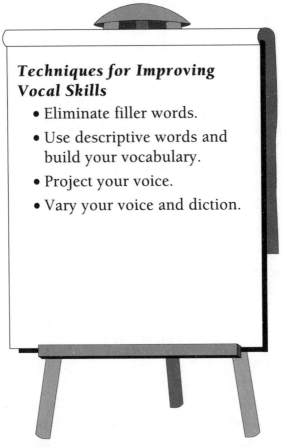

Techniques for Improving Vocal Skills

- Eliminate filler words.
- Use descriptive words and build your vocabulary.
- Project your voice.
- Vary your voice and diction.

Eliminate filler words.

Record yourself while you speak on the phone and every time you give a presentation. Listen for the filler words and begin to weed them out of your speech.

Try putting a bright, colored dot on your watch face to remind you to listen during the day for the use of fillers.

When you begin to speak, rather than saying "uh" (as some people do before almost every phrase or when giving their name and phone number), simply pause. You will sound more articulate and powerful.

Use descriptive words and build your vocabulary.

Listen to your word usage. Can you use more descriptive and creative expressions?

Take advantage of the grammar books or classes that are available to brush up on the basics to help you feel more confident.

Listen to a vocabulary-building cassette tape.

Attend a Toastmasters meeting. Most Toastmasters clubs have a grammarian who listens for correct and incorrect uses of grammar and introduces a new "word of the week" to help build vocabularies.

Project your voice.

Use more air as you speak. Breathe from your diaphragm to increase your intensity and volume.

Open your mouth and move your lips more vigorously. Practice moving your chin up and down by lightly grasping your chin with your fingers. See if you can move the lower jaw up and down and back and forth. Practice moving your chin and relaxing your jaw for less tension and more volume when you speak.

Slow down (especially when using a microphone). The larger the room in which you are speaking, the longer it will take for your voice to travel.

Vary your voice and diction.

To lower your pitch: Sit in a chair and recite your favorite poem or nursery rhyme (such as "Twinkle, Twinkle Little Star"). Begin from an upright seated posture. Then proceed to lean forward as you speak, bending at the waist, until you can bend no farther. Did you hear your vocal pitch drop to a lower level as you spoke? When you lean forward you are forcing yourself to breathe diaphragmatically. When you speak from your diaphragm, you are in your natural pitch.

To lessen nasality: Retraining the tongue can lessen nasality. Some voice coaches recommend exercises such as this: Place a cork or a large plastic pen (such as a plastic highlighter) in your mouth so that the cork or pen rests on your tongue. Proceed by reading aloud. When you remove the pen, talking seems much easier. You'll become more aware of how to control your tongue.

To enunciate more clearly: Tongue twisters have been around for a long time. Peter Piper was first published in England in 1674 in a book titled Peter Piper's Practical Principles of Plain and Perfect Pronunciation.

Try reading the following twisters over and over again while increasing your pace as you go. You will be practicing your precision as a speaker and developing your ability to enunciate well.

Peter Piper picked a peck of pickled peppers.
Did Peter Piper pick a peck of pickled peppers?
If Peter Piper picked a peck of pickled peppers,
Where's the peck of pickled peppers Peter Piper picked?

All I want is a proper cup of coffee
Made in a proper copper coffee pot.
You can believe it or not,
But I just want a cup of coffee
In a proper coffee pot.
Tin coffee pots
Or iron coffee pots
Are of no use to me. If I can't have
A proper cup of coffee
In a proper copper coffee pot,
I'll have a cup of tea!

Betty Botter bought some butter.
"But," she said, "the butter's bitter.
If I put it in my batter,
It will make my batter bitter.
But a bit of better butter—
That would make my batter better."
So she bought a bit of butter,
Better than her bitter butter.
And she put it in her batter,
And the batter was not bitter.
So 'twas better Betty Botter
Bought a bit of better butter.

If neither he sells seashells,
Nor she sells seashells,
Who shall sell seashells?
Shall seashells be sold?

Our Joe wants to know if your Joe will lend our Joe your Joe's banjo.
If your Joe won't lend our Joe your Joe's banjo, our Joe won't lend your Joe our Joe's banjo when our Joe has a banjo!

If Roland Reynolds rolled a round roll around a round room,
Where is the round roll which Roland Reynolds rolled around the room?

Granny gray goose greedily gobbled golden grain in Graham's gabled granary.

Radio and television personalities have to practice their articulation by working on the *plosive sounds*. Plosives are caused by the following letters:

b (as in ta*b*)
ch (as in lur*ch*)
d (as in dee*d*)
g (as in di*g*)

j (as in ju*d*ge)

k (as in sa*ck*)

p (as in li*p*)

t (as in boo*t*)

When these letters come at the end of a word, there is an explosion of air that adds emphasis and crispness to your speech.

Listen to radio announcers, television news reporters, and commercial voice-overs with a careful ear. Listen for the emphasis and clarity caused by the plosive sounds.

Recite the following while noticing the plosive influence.

A tooter who tooted a flute
Tried to tutor two tutors to toot.
Said the two to their tutor,
"Is it harder to toot or
To tutor two tutors to toot?"

Weak writers want white ruled writing paper.

I was looking back
To see if she was looking back
To see if I was looking back
To see if she was looking back at me.

Tell me, Todd, what was it that brought you to the tower?"

Did Donald donate to the dedication fund?

The kid hid under the bed to hide from the bad Fred.

Let us go gather lettuce,
Whether the weather will let us or not.

The fish and chop shop's chips are soft chips.

A haddock!
A haddock!
A black-spotted haddock!
A black spot
On the black back
Of a black-spotted haddock!

Mee May Mah Moh Moo
Nee Nay Nah Noh Noo
Tee Tay Tah Toh Too
Dee Day Dah Doh Doo
Heed Hayd Hahd Hohd Hood
Heet Hayt Hite Hoht Hoot
Hee-tee Hay-tay Hah-tah Hot-toh Hoo-too

 Watch news reporters and professional speakers to observe how they have been trained to speak. Reading aloud to your spouse, children, friends, or significant other is a fantastic way to practice public speaking, projection techniques, and vocal variety. Children's books are especially good for practicing your skills. Joining a reading club or becoming a member of a story-telling group would provide even more opportunities.

Speaking on the Telephone

Tips for the Telephone
- Project friendliness (smile).
- Project your voice.
- Vary vocal pitch and rate.
- Use telephone etiquette.
- Leave effective messages.

Positive vocal qualities are important even when speaking on the telephone. You convey the majority of your message over the phone by how you sound. You want to sound clear, vibrant, energetic, and friendly. You want to come across as an adult with authority and power, yet approachable and open. Your telephone voice can be enhanced by incorporating these positive vocal qualities and techniques.

Project friendliness.

To sound friendly on the telephone, remember to smile. Many telemarketing firms place mirrors in front of each telephone operator as a reminder to smile. A smile is a universal message of friendliness. People can easily hear a smile in your voice.

Project your voice.

If you want to increase your vocal projection and volume over the phone, try standing up while you talk. You will be able to breathe more easily if you are not sitting with a slumped posture. You will also sound more energetic.

Vary vocal pitch and rate.

Vary your pitch and rate as you speak to add more interest and vitality to your words. Give words meaning. For example, if you say, "It's been so long since I've talked with you," make the word *long* sound *long* by elongating it. If you say the word *soft*, make it sound soft. Begin to notice what words can be given life for extra emphasis and meaning.

Use telephone etiquette.

Telephone etiquette is an essential skill for the polished communicator. The following tips for calling and leaving messages will project you as a professional, considerate, and articulate caller.

- Avoid eating, chewing gum, or drinking while on the phone.
- Identify yourself by stating your full name and, if appropriate, your company or whom you are representing. This saves time and immediately tells the person you are calling who you are, sending a message

of confidence about you to the receiver. Remember to smile and project your voice. To sound more energetic or powerful, stand up.

- Ask the person, "Is this a good time for you?" If the person sounds rushed, busy, or preoccupied, offer to call back at a more convenient time. Find out when would be the best time to call back. The caller will appreciate your consideration, and you will probably have a better interaction during your follow-up call as a result.

- Take notes during the conversation.

- Thank the person you have called. Demonstrate an appreciation for someone allowing you to interrupt their day, especially if you are calling for information, advice, or business purposes. Follow through on what you say you will do.

Leave effective messages.

Don't forget telephone etiquette when you must leave a message. Countless times I have received messages from people whom I do not know well and who identify themselves by first name only. When I worked in the pharmaceutical sales field, I would receive several messages each day. Some people would leave a message on my answering machine such as, "Hi, this is Diana at the doctor's office. Would you give me a call when you get in?" The caller didn't let me know: (1) her full name, (2) the name of the doctor she represented, (3) the purpose of the call, or (4) the telephone number. Phone messages such as the one from "Diana" are very frustrating to receive because I know at least ten Dianas. When I worked in the pharmaceutical field, I called on more than five hundred physicians.

Receiving a Complaint Call

- Listen carefully.
- Take notes.
- Use the person's name courteously.
- Express your interest in the problem.
- Ask questions.
- Show your concern.
- Apologize.
- Explain what you will do to remedy the situation.
- Take the appropriate action.
- Follow up.

Leaving a Message

- Before you place a call, plan what you are going to say and anticipate the possibility of reaching an answering machine rather than the person.
- Speak clearly and slowly.
- State your full name (even if the person knows you).
- Tell the time and date of your call.
- State the purpose of your call.
- Give the best time to return your call, to reduce the time playing telephone tag.
- Leave your phone number even if you know the person has it. (The message might be picked up by a person who is out of town, or away from the office, and does not have your number on hand.) State your phone number at the speed it would take you to write it so that the listener does not have to replay your message several times to get the correct number.

Evaluate Your Voice

Here's an opportunity to evaluate your voice. Tape record yourself while talking on the telephone to a friend or client. (Record only your side of the conversation.) You will then hear a good representation of what you sound like to others. Listen to the tape and answer these questions:

- ☐ Did you speak clearly so that you were easily understood?

- ☐ Did you hear the beginnings and endings of words such as them, going, doing, being, want to, could you, rather than 'em, goin', doin', bein', wanna, cudja?

- ☐ How was your rate of speech? Fast? Slow? Varied?

- ☐ How was your vocal variety? Varied? Energetic? Lethargic? Harsh?

- ☐ How did your tone sound? Soft? Loud? Monotone? Nervous? Tired? Nasal? Negative? Positive?

- ☐ How did your pitch sound? Too high? Too low? Unnatural?

- ☐ Did your voice fade out at the end of your sentences or phrases?

- ☐ Did you run out of breath or hear yourself sigh?

- ☐ Did you hear yourself using good attending (listening) skills such as uh-huh, um, yes, oh, really?

- ☐ Did you emphasize certain words for extra punch?

- ☐ Did you hear many unwanted fillers in your speech? (uh, um, er, like, you know)

- ☐ Did you hear a tongue click? (Pssst sound)

- ☐ Did you display any nervous mannerisms such as coughing or throat clearing?

- ☐ Could you hear a smile (not a giggle) in your voice?

- ☐ Did you interrupt, or were you often interrupted?

Summarize your evaluation on Work Sheet 5. Recognize your strong areas and note the areas you would like to improve. Then practice the exercises provided in this chapter, which will help you continue developing your vocal qualities.

Work Sheet 5
Evaluate Your Voice

What are your positive vocal qualities?

What did you hear that you would like to change or improve upon?

Remember, don't be too hard on yourself. Most of us don't like to hear our own voices at first. Avoid saying, "Oh, I hate the way I sound." Find the positives in your vocal style and then decide to build on that foundation. Give yourself credit for being willing to tape record yourself and to develop the vocal qualities you want.

For example, you may think that your pitch was too high, too soft, and did not have the sound of authority. Tell yourself what you are going to do to make the changes you want. "I'm going to work on lowering my pitch, increasing my volume, and learning to speak with authority by eliminating the giggling, the fillers, and the breathiness from my speech patterns." (Tell yourself what you want, not what you don't want.)

Summary

The way you speak conveys a great deal about yourself. You can continually develop your voice, whether you are conversing on the phone, speaking with friends, or participating in a business meeting.

Tape recording yourself, observing proficient speakers, practicing the qualities you want to incorporate into your voice, and putting vocal vitality into your words will heighten your confidence. In turn, that confidence will attract a more attentive audience.

3

Becoming a Charmed Listener

If you are not a charming conversationalist, you may still be a big hit as a charmed listener.

Being a good listener does not just mean waiting until it is your turn to speak. It means really listening to what another person has to say. While hearing is an innate ability, listening is a learned skill.

In the previous chapter we saw that *interrupting while others are talking* was listed as the most annoying trait. Whether you are speaking face to face or by telephone or other electronic medium, you must exercise skill and courtesy as a listener.

Develop Listening Skills

Consider the characteristics of a poor listener.

Characteristics of a Poor Listener
- Talks too much and much too often.
- Shows no interest or energy.
- Interested only when he or she gets to speak.
- Interrupts often.
- Asks no questions.
- Uses the words *I*, *me*, and *my* constantly.
- Distracted easily.
- Seems to be insensitive to others.
- Argues easily.
- Tunes out the other person if delivery is poor or slow.
- Disinterested body language.

Studies show that Americans spend 80 percent of their waking hours communicating, 45 percent of which is spent listening. We spend more time listening than using any other form of communication. Yet we listen at only 25 percent of our ability.

In business, listening is recognized as the most important managerial skill, yet it is the communication skill that is taught the least.

The four basic communication skills are *learned* in the following order:

Listening Speaking Reading Writing

The four basic communication skills are *used* in the following order:

Listening (45 percent)

Speaking (30 percent)

Reading (16 percent)

Writing (9 percent)

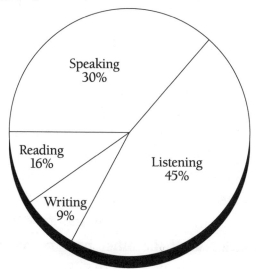

The amount of training given to the four basic communication skills is as follows:

Listening (least)

Speaking (next least)

Reading (second most)

Writing (most)

When listening skills are taught in universities, colleges, and schools, comprehension rises dramatically. Listening can be enhanced, and the benefits are measurable and positive.

Tips for More Effective Listening

- In order to listen, you have to stop talking.
- Listen actively so that you can understand the other person's point of view. Have empathy.
- Look and act interested in what the person is saying. For example, maintain eye contact and avoid tapping your pen or looking at your watch.
- Ask appropriate questions to demonstrate interest and to show that you are listening.
- Avoid jumping to a conclusion or judgment. Wait to hear the story.
- Listen for content and feelings.
- Respond to the feelings of the other person and avoid turning the conversation to your own situation.
- Be patient and do not interrupt. Allow pauses and time for response. (Introverts take longer to speak up than extroverts.)
- Observe nonverbal behavior and look for clues.
- Summarize what the other person has said to show that you are listening and to check for understanding.

Try It Now

The following activities will help you check your listening strengths and determine areas to develop.

1. The next time you attend a lecture, class, meeting, or other type of presentation, compare your notes with a colleague or friend afterward. Consider these questions:
   - What was important to you?
   - What was important to the other person?
   - What do you both think were the important messages from the speaker's standpoint?
   - Which of you retained the most information? What listening skills helped to increase retention?
2. Use Work Sheet 6 to evaluate your listening practices or give it to a friend to evaluate you. It is useful to compare your self-assessment with other people's perceptions.
3. Summarize your evaluation. Recognize your strong areas and note the areas you would like to improve. Practice the techniques provided in this chapter to continue developing your listening skills.
   - What are your positive listening behaviors?
   - What would you like to change or improve?

Summary

The way you speak and listen conveys a great deal about yourself. You can develop your listening and vocal skills during every conversation, whether on the phone, at the dinner table, or at a meeting.

Human beings tend to agree with people they like. It's interesting to note that 80 percent of people who fail on the job usually fail because of their inability to get along well with people.

It's also interesting to note that people tend to like other people who will listen to them. If you listen, you will increase your ability to learn, you will enhance your relationships, and you will be more likable. Practicing good listening and speaking will enhance all of your relationships.

Work Sheet 6
Check Out Your Listening Skills

	Yes	No
1. Are you careful not to dominate the conversation?	☐	☐
2. Do you seek to understand the other person's point of view?	☐	☐
3. Do you look and act interested in what the person is saying?	☐	☐
4. Do you maintain eye contact?	☐	☐
5. Do you avoid distractions like tapping your pen or looking at your watch?	☐	☐
6. Do you ask appropriate questions?	☐	☐
7. Do you avoid jumping to a conclusion or judgment?	☐	☐
8. Do you listen for content and feelings?	☐	☐
9. Do you respond to the feelings of the other person and avoid turning the conversation to your own situation?	☐	☐
10. Are you patient, allowing pauses and time for response?	☐	☐
11. Do you observe nonverbal behavior for clues?	☐	☐
12. Do you help summarize what the other person has said to check for understanding?	☐	☐

4

Body Language: The Hidden Communicator

He who knows that power is inborn…and so perceiving, throws himself unhesitatingly on his thought, instantly rights himself, stands in the erect position, commands his limbs, works miracles.

Ralph Waldo Emerson

Body language is 55 percent of any message. Body language says much more than words. You may have heard this expression: The way you say what you say and the way you look when you say it speaks so loudly that I can't hear what it is that you're saying! Your gestures and body language are five times more powerful than your verbal message. If your body language and your words are inconsistent, people will believe your body.

If I were to say, "Oh, I'm sure I can do that job," and at the same time fidgeted with my fingers, spoke with my head down, made no eye contact, slumped my posture, shuffled my feet, and spoke softly and timidly, would you believe me? Of course not. If, however, I spoke with my head up, made eye contact, stood erect, did not fidget, firmly planted my feet, and spoke with enthusiasm and projection, you *would* believe me. By simply changing your posture, mannerisms, and movement, you can communicate with more credibility and power.

In 1979, I saw a videotape of myself sitting with my legs crossed at the knee, my hands folded in my lap, elbows tightly held against my sides, and my ankles wrapped around the leg of a chair. It was not the picture of confidence that I wanted to portray. Seeing myself on video, I realized how I did *not* want to look. Videotape is a powerful tool in helping us learn what we need to change. In my seminars and training sessions, I show many pictures and videos of models, actors, and everyday people to demonstrate how we can observe in others what we admire or see as ineffective.

Most people admire famous actors, celebrities, or motivational speakers who have the ability to communicate with confidence, sincerity, friendliness, enthusiasm, and more. You can have those same qualities, too, if you choose. Remember the adage "If it is to be, it's up to me." To develop the qualities you want in yourself you must first mentally decide what you want to project. Then start projecting that image through your body language.

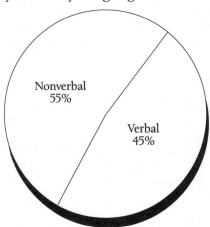

Use Body Language to Communicate

Body Language Techniques

- Increase your physical space.
- Keep your posture erect and your chin up.
- Plant yourself evenly on both feet.
- Move deliberately.
- Relax your hands at your sides.
- Eliminate distracting items.
- Create congruence with your message.

Increase your physical space.

Natasha Josefowitz, author of *Paths to Power*, said that "powerful people take up space." Think about Wonder Woman or Superman. They physically took up space by standing with their feet apart, heads up, and their hands on their hips. Unfortunately, many of us were taught to take up the least amount of space possible. Most women learn to sit with legs primly crossed and hands clasped tightly in their laps. Practice increasing your space.

Observe actors and models. See how they have been trained to *take up space.* Begin to increase your physical space by keeping more space between your elbows and body. For example, if your hands are together, keep them at waist level. Your elbows will naturally extend outward from your body and will create a more powerful stance.

Keep your posture erect and your chin up.

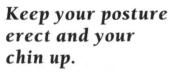

Your posture communicates how you feel about yourself. Keeping your posture erect and your chin up conveys a sense of energy and confidence. Think about how news reporter Diane Sawyer holds her head. She projects a very confident image with her stance. Be careful not to hold your head so

high that you appear aloof or arrogant. Pull your shoulders back and keep your spine straight but not stiff.

Plant yourself evenly on both feet.

When standing and speaking before a group place your feet apart about eight to twelve inches, depending on your height. *Plant* yourself the way actors do with your weight evenly distributed on both feet. If you shift your weight from foot to foot, you will look less balanced and less powerful. If you are giving a presentation and you want to appeal for action from the audience, place one foot forward and put more weight on your front foot. This will make you look like you are reaching out to others. Then return to the even stance.

Move deliberately.

Movement is an effective way to support and visually convey your message. The key is to avoid pacing or too much movement and balance a firm stance with deliberate movements. I once evaluated a professional speaker known for his high energy. He left me, and others, feeling exhausted because of his nonstop action. To me, he appeared as a caged tiger. He paced incessantly. His movement was a distraction instead of a contributor to his message. If he had moved from side to side to coincide with his transition statements, his movement would have clearly enhanced the meaning of his words. A good technique is to start center stage, move right as you make your first point, return to the center, and then move left as you make your second point, and so forth. Finally, return to the center as you conclude your speech.

Relax your hands at your sides.

Learn to stand with your hands relaxed at your sides. Many people find this difficult to do. It can be learned. If you learn to relax without holding on to anything, you will appear to be more confident. For some people, it is a tough challenge to keep their hands out of their pockets. Allow your hands to be free so that your gestures can come easily and look more natural. Body language should always look natural, not stiff and mechanical. A rule of thumb is to exaggerate your gestures with groups of more than fifty.

Gestures should occur at the waist level or above. Unfortunately, without a crutch to hold onto, many people resort to the fig leaf or the reverse fig leaf pose (hands together and dropping them, fully extended in front of your body or in the reverse manner behind you). In my programs I use photographs from advertisements to demonstrate positive and negative body language. One suit ad, for example, shows a man standing in the fig leaf position, his head down, feet close together, and eyes cast downward. When I ask the audience to describe the man, I inevitably hear adjectives such as depressed, dejected, sad, unhappy, morose, fearful, not confident, low self-esteem, and mournful. Never do I hear positive comments. The fig leaf posture does not communicate a powerful message.

Eliminate distracting items.

Fidgeting is a distraction and is perceived as nervousness and lack of self-assurance. At meetings, it's best to avoid holding pens, paper clips, or any item that you might absentmindedly play with. Whatever a speaker holds becomes fascinating to the audience. Avoid having anything in your pockets that rattles. Some people are especially fond of jingling the change in their pockets. It becomes a habit and distracts from what is being said. Empty your pockets of money, wallets, pens, and keys before a presentation. It's okay to have one hand in your pocket to portray a relaxed appearance, but both hands in your pockets limits your gestures and appears too casual.

Create congruence with your message.

Always make your body language consistent with your message. If your body language is not in sync with your words, people will believe your body language. For example, while I was waiting to speak to a convention group, I listened to a sales manager conclude a presentation with an inconsistent message. The manager was saying, "Yes, you can reach your goals. Yes, you can make it to the top!" However, while he was speaking the words he was also shaking his head no. The unspoken message was "No, you really can't." I saw a similar occurrence in the debate between the candidates for the 1990 governor's race in California. As Dianne Feinstein delivered her summary statement, she said, "I support 'Big Green.'" But as she spoke the words, she shook her head to the contrary. Her words were inconsistent with her message.

Crossed arms can convey a closed or unreceptive mind. To be perceived as a good listener, have face-to-face body language without crossed arms. Leaning forward and tilting the head slightly gives the impression that you are interested in what is being said. In sales, it is very difficult to get a positive response from a customer who is leaning back with his or her arms and legs crossed. Until the person's arms and legs are uncrossed and the person leans forward, it is unlikely that the sale will take place.

Tilting your head slightly is a positive gesture when listening; but when speaking it is not perceived as positive or powerful. Tilting your head when listening makes you appear more thoughtful and attentive. However, if you saw news anchors Dan Rather, Tom Brokaw, or Peter Jennings tilting their heads back and forth while reporting, you would probably think it strange. Keep your head up and untilted whenever you want to come across with authority and power when speaking or presenting.

The most powerful gesture you can use is the so-called *steeple* gesture. Steepling is finger tips to finger tips with the palms apart and the fingers pointed outward or upward, or the hands loosely clasped with the index fingers pointing and thumbs touching. While seated, you may rest your arms on a table (midway between the elbows and wrists) and hold your hands in the steeple formation. This gesture is one of the best negotiating postures that you can use. Watch for this gesture especially when observing politicians, CEOs, and attorneys.

Try It Now

The following exercises will help you develop your body language. You will need a quiet place and some uninterrupted time to play with these techniques. Refer to the Body Language Techniques on page 57.

Close your eyes and imagine a person that you like and admire—someone you think of as a good communicator. Who came to mind? What qualities does that person have that you like and admire?

Decide what you want to project and then practice projecting that image through your body language. The following exercises will show you how to communicate through posture and mannerisms.

You might want to videotape yourself doing the exercises to see how you look. Practice until you feel comfortable, using the video as feedback. Then, tape yourself going through the entire session as you want to appear. Plant that image in your memory.

- Use affirmations to record supportive thoughts.
  For example:
  I am comfortable taking up more physical space.
  I stand straight with my chin up and my feet firmly placed.
  When I speak I am relaxed and natural.
  I move effectively with purpose and power.
- Increase your physical space.
  Extend your elbows outward from your body. See how it looks in a mirror or on videotape.
  Create a neutral posture by dropping one hand at your side and standing with your other hand at waist level, elbow bent.
  Sit in a chair. Keep your elbows away from your body. Rest your arms (elbows outward) on the arms of the chair. (A chair without arms has been called a *powerless chair*.)
- Keep your posture erect and your chin up.
  To convey confidence, imagine a string pulling the top of your head up. Pull yourself up, chin forward, relaxing your shoulders backward. Check out your image. Is your head so high that you appear aloof or arrogant? Relax it a little. Keep your spine straight but not stiff.

- Plant yourself evenly on both feet.

    Place your feet apart about eight to twelve inches, depending on your height. *Plant* yourself with your weight evenly distributed on both feet. Now shift your weight from foot to foot. Do you feel and look less balanced and less powerful?

    Standing, place one foot forward and put more weight on your front foot. Do you look as if you are appealing to others? Now return to the even stance and observe how it looks.

- Move deliberately.

    Pace back and forth in front of a mirror or camera to see and feel how it looks. Talk out loud as you move, as if you are addressing a group.

- Relax your hands at your sides.

    Allow your hands to be free so that your gestures will come easily and look more natural. It may take some practice to allow your hands to relax.

    Take the fig leaf pose, with hands together dropped fully extended in front of your body. Now hold this position and recite "Mary Had a Little Lamb." Recite the poem again with your hands moving naturally in gestures. Observe how it looks.

    Try the reverse fig leaf position with your hands held behind you. Let your head droop and put your feet close together. How does this look? Now place your hands at your sides with your feet apart and your head upright. See the difference.

    Cross your arms as you try to appeal to an imaginary group to accept your proposal. Observe how it looks. Unfold your arms and tilt your head slightly as you reiterate the benefits. See how it might appear reflective and inactive.

- Eliminate distracting items.

    Fiddle with an earring, change in your pocket, or a pen and notice how distracting this is. Now free your hands and try the next exercise.

- Create congruence with your message.

    Close your eyes and imagine someone you like and admire.

    Affirm your ability to project yourself similarly. Think about your physical space. Hold yourself upright and breathe deeply. Notice your feet; get a firm stance. Relax your hands by your sides. Conduct an imaginary conversation and move your body naturally but deliberately to convey the words.

 Observe actors and models and see how they have been trained to move confidently. Professional coaching and evaluation can also provide immeasurable help in learning to project the image that you want to convey.

Communicate With Eye Contact

As mentioned previously, eye contact makes up about 55 percent of the nonverbal part of a message. Most people think that when a person speaks without making eye contact that he or she is

- Lying
- Shy
- Not confident
- Not trustworthy
- Uncaring
- Distracted
- Embarrassed

- Shifty
- Hiding something

Most comments about lack of eye contact are negative or unfavorable. Good communicators and good listeners develop positive eye contact with other people. Michael Gelb said, "Eye contact is a humanizing element in an often impersonal world."

Eye contact is an important part of being perceived as an honest, sincere, and confident person. People can and do make assumptions about others who cannot make eye contact. The most common assumption is that lack of eye contact means lack of honesty. Most employers report that they would hesitate to hire a person who failed to look them in the eye. Developing good eye contact promotes a positive self-image.

Eye Contact Techniques

- Get control of your audience right away.
- Look at every section of the audience and maintain eye contact.

Get control of your audience right away.

When you make a presentation, wait until you have control of your audience before you start your message. Give the audience a few seconds to settle down. Wait for any talking and movement to stop before your opening. Eye contact with the audience will communicate that you want their attention.

Not long ago I was hired by an attorney to observe him in court to assess his effectiveness as a communicator. The attorney had an excellent case to present. He was well prepared, articulate, and professionally attired. During his opening argument, however, when the critical information regarding the case was presented to the jury, the attorney failed to maintain control of the jury through eye contact.

As the attorney began to speak, the bailiff in the court-room walked in front of the lawyer and began to distribute "Jury Member" badges to every member of the jury. As the box of badges was passed from person to person, each juror took a badge, looked it over, looked at the next juror to see where he or she had clipped the badge, tried the badge on, and then finally looked backed to the attorney who was continuing to speak. Next, the bailiff walked back across the room and retrieved a stack of steno pads and proceeded to pass in front of the speaking attorney again. The jurors were distracted for another two minutes. The third and final time the bailiff walked back and forth across the courtroom he brought twelve sharpened pencils to the jurors.

By the time the jurors had their name badges, notepads, and pencils, the attorney had finished his opening remarks. His chance of winning his case was also finished. He lost the case because he had failed to "grab the audience" in the vital first few minutes of his presentation.

The attorney was amazed at my observations. He had been unaware of what the bailiff had been doing. The lawyer was so involved with what *he* was saying and doing that he had been oblivious to the fact that his audience was completely distracted. I recommended to the lawyer that he *always* wait until the jurors have their materials before proceeding with his opening arguments. In his next case, the following week, he did just that and won a substantial judgment for his client. After the trial, he polled the jurors about his communication skills. The jurors said that, without a doubt, he had controlled the action in the courtroom by simply stopping whenever a distraction occurred and making sure that everyone was able to hear his message.

The attorney should have simply said, "Ladies and gentlemen of the jury, what I have to say is so important that I don't want you to miss a single word. I'm going to wait until you have all of your materials before I proceed." Then the jury would have been eagerly waiting to hear every word of the opening argument. It's the same with any presentation. Give the audience a few seconds to settle down before your opening. Eye contact with the audience will communicate that you want their attention. Pausing and waiting for control will send a message of power.

Look at every section of the audience and maintain eye contact.

It is important to include everyone as equally as possible and to hold your eye contact with each person with whom you are speaking.

When speaking before a group, look at every section of the audience. Look people in the eye. Some speech coaches advise people to look over the heads of the audience, but I think that is terrible advice. I know whether someone is looking over my head or into my eyes. When you are speaking, you will get feedback by "reading" your audience. You will know if someone is tracking with you, agreeing, not comprehending, or getting confused. All of that feedback comes by way of reading other people through eye contact and facial expressions.

The odds are 160:1 that if a person doesn't look at you when speaking, he or she isn't listening either. Eye contact is essential to being perceived as a good listener. Think about how lack of eye contact impresses you. Have you ever felt excluded from a conversation because of lack of eye contact? When talking to someone, have you ever felt that the person was observing other people rather than listening to you? Most people want to end a conversation if they do not feel wanted. Use positive eye contact to include the audience in your presentation.

Summary

Sandy Linver, in her book *Speak Easy*, claims, "Using your body to release energy is a learned activity. If you are not used to expressing yourself physically, you can learn to do it." Train yourself to speak the same language with your words and body. Positive body language and eye contact will allow you to be perceived as a polished communicator.

5

Projecting a
Positive Image

Dress shabbily and people will remember the outfit. Dress elegantly and people will remember the person.

Paraphrased, from Coco Chanel

several years ago I ran into a friend at a clothing boutique. With excitement she told me that she was shopping for an outfit to wear to a White House reception and dinner. I asked her what type of outfit she was looking for. She responded, "I haven't decided whether I want to look good or want to be remembered!"

I think it's possible to look good *and* be remembered at the same time. Consistently looking your best sends a message to others that you respect yourself. Denis Waitley, author of *The Psychology of Winning*, advises people "to dress and look your best at all times regardless of pressure from your friends and peers. Personal grooming and lifestyle appearance provide an instantaneous projection on the surface of how you feel inside about yourself."

Teachers often report that students are more well behaved and seem more confident on the day that school pictures are taken because they are carefully dressed and well groomed. Like it or not, the way we dress and look does affect our performance, the way we feel about ourselves, and the way others respond to us.

This chapter offers some suggestions for image and dress to help you come across as a more powerful communicator with polish and pizazz. These are only suggestions, and they mainly relate to the average American business person. Obviously, the image of a corporate business executive is different from a coach. And an elementary school teacher would not dress the same as a high-fashion model. Ultimately you have to decide what works best for you in your particular field and provides the image you wish to convey to others.

Think about how good you feel when you wear an outfit that you especially like—an outfit that people compliment you for. It may be a jacket that fits you well, or a shirt or blouse in a color that makes you feel energetic and positive.

Now think about an outfit that you still wonder why you bought it. Perhaps it was on sale and you liked the designer, the fabric, and the price but you had second thoughts after getting the outfit home. Maybe you knew how good it would look on someone else and you hoped it would work the same magic on you.

Purchase clothing and accessories carefully. Ask for the advice of a personal shopper or image consultant if you need help. Classes and workshops are also available for learning how to make good decisions about your wardrobe investments.

Tips for Looking Your Best

Most rules apply to both men and women. A commonsense approach will ensure that you look professional and in control, which will make you feel the same way.

Accessories

- Accessories should be simple and not distracting. You should wear no more than one ring on each hand. Anything too flashy may be perceived negatively by an audience.

- Be consistent. Wear gold or silver but not both. Wear one color or the other.

- Women should avoid wearing jewelry that makes noise (bangle or charm bracelets, for example), especially when giving a presentation. Multiple-link or chain necklaces that might hit a lavaliere (lapel) microphone may also be a problem.

- Women should wear earrings that are large enough to be seen from across the room (at least the size of a quarter coin). When making a presentation to an audience, avoid wearing dangling earrings that move. Speech coach Dorothy Sarnoff has said, "they have a life of their own" and the audience will be distracted by their movement each time you move your head.

- If you wear a scarf or pocket-handkerchief, make certain it is anchored and will stay in place so that you do not have to rearrange it every few minutes.

- Pocket-handkerchiefs coordinated with a tie give a dressier, more finished look.

- Wear a belt for a finished look.

- Carry a quality leather handbag or attaché case that is not too large. If you carry an attaché case, do not also carry a purse. Use one or the other. You may want to put a small bag inside your attaché for personal items.

- Men's ties should be current but not trendy. It's always best to err on the side of being conservative.

- Wear socks, stockings, or pantyhose that do not distract. Avoid patterns and textures. (It's a good idea for women to carry an extra pair of stockings with them in case of a run.)
- Men's socks should cover the calf so that none of your leg shows when you are seated. Do not wear light socks with dark pants.

Shoes

- Buy quality shoes—the best you can afford. Keep them freshly polished and in good repair. If you are speaking on a raised platform, people will especially notice your shoes.
- The best shoe style for women is a closed-toe, closed-heel, classic leather pump with a modest heel. Avoid wearing shoes with ankle straps. The strap breaks the line of sight and makes you look shorter and more childlike.
- Wear shoes that are as dark or darker than your hemline. You want a dark base, or anchor, so that people will not be distracted by your shoes. For example, wearing white shoes with a dark suit would cause people to notice your shoes more than your outfit.
- Shoe clips should be the same gold or silver tone that you wear in your jewelry.

Clothing

- Dress appropriately for the occasion. When asked about dressing to create a positive image, a psychologist responded, "There is no right or wrong way to dress. There is only an appropriate way to dress." For example, avoid formal or evening dress during the day (tuxedos, sequins, and rhinestones are inappropriate for daytime).

- As the speaker or presenter you should be the best dressed person in the audience. (This doesn't mean matching price tags or designer labels. It simply means that if people in the audience are in dressy suits, you should be dressed in a similar fashion.)

- For greater authority and power, a woman should wear a jacket. Jackets are one of your best investments.

- Buy quality fabrics. Think of quality clothing as an investment. Classic outfits made of good fabric will last for years and will be well worth the money. (It's better to have fewer outfits that are long lasting than many outfits that are trendy and do not wear well.)

- Buy simple, timeless, yet elegant clothing. You can dress up a suit with accessories and change the look by changing the color of the blouse or shirt or by adding a scarf or pocket-handkerchief. A navy suit, for example, provides a base for countless looks.

- Solid colors and subtle patterns give a look of power. A dark suit is the most powerful look for business. (Picture a woman wearing a dark navy blue suit with a red silk blouse standing next to a woman in a pale pink suit with a white blouse. Who looks more powerful? Note that IBM's "signature" suit is navy blue.)

- Wear accent colors that enhance your appearance. (Some men look great in light pink shirts.)

- Avoid wearing clothing that conveys an overly young look for your age (for example, ruffles, bows, or a fish tie). This look will not send a message of competence.

- Have clothing tailored so that the length of your sleeves and pants or skirt are correct.

- Women should wear their hemlines at the knee or below. According to image consultant Carol Ann Pearce, "Don't go above the knee with a hemline unless your legs are terrific and the length allows only a modest glimpse."

- Power dress appropriately. Although John Malloy's *The Woman's Dress for Success Book* has some excellent suggestions, it is no longer recommended that women wear pinstriped suits and ties. Watch for good role models. Some excellent examples of power dressing can be seen by watching news anchors such as Connie Chung, or programs such as *L.A. Law*. These wardrobes usually consist of conservative suits and jewelry with classic silk blouses and pocket squares.

Cosmetics

- If you need help in buying the right makeup, go to a makeup artist or attend a class on color, products, and application.

- Makeup can enhance any woman's appearance. Even a small amount can have positive impact. No make-up is generally too plain for business, whereas too much makeup sends a negative message. (When speaking before an audience or making a television appearance, extra makeup will be needed.)

- Have your nails manicured before important presentations or events. Nails should not be too long, and nail polish should not be too bright. You don't want your nails to be a distraction.

- Acrylic nails make noise when they click together. Be cautious about drumming your nails on a table or lectern. Many professional speakers have been told that their nails were distracting.

Hair

- Your hair cut should be professionally done and cut in a style that is neat and not trendy. You do not want people to notice your haircut and miss your message. Women's hair should be shoulder length or above. (When I took the John Robert Powers Professional Course I had long hair. The first thing I was advised to do was cut my hair.)

- Avoid a hairstyle that falls forward into your face or bangs that are too long. If you are constantly brushing back your hair with your hand, your hairstyle will serve as a distraction.

Color

- Wear colors that make you feel good and ones that people compliment you for wearing. Most people look especially good in certain colors. Notice how you feel and how others respond to you when you are wearing different colors. You might want to have your colors analyzed by a color expert.

- Wear darker colors for a more powerful look. Black is the most powerful color of all. (Think of black-tie events and the look of a tuxedo or elegant black dress.) As a speaker it's best to wear darker colors as a base. For example, wear a dark-colored skirt with dark shoes and the lighter, brighter colors on the upper half of your body. This will draw your audience's attention upward toward your face.

- If you are making a television or media appearance, avoid wearing black and white. Bright solid colors are better—colors such as teal, red, or royal blue look good on camera.

- Navy blue is referred to as a *sincere* color and tests well with employers and audiences. Recall what almost all presidential candidates have worn during debates: "navy blue suit, a white shirt, and a red and navy tie. A brown suit should be avoided because it does not spell *power*.

- Bright colors with a contrasting suit or blouse go well together. Think of a navy blue suit with a red silk blouse, a crisp white shirt, or a hot-pink blouse.

- Different colors send different messages. For example, teal is considered the color of the communicator. Bright yellow is associated with learning, perhaps because color experts say it is the fastest color for your eye to see. Red sends a message of energy, while orange may send a negative signal of agitation. Orange is avoided in prisons and mental institutions, whereas pale blue and pink colors are used. Colors definitely cause a reaction in all of us. Make certain the colors you select are right for you and are sending the message you want to convey.

- When you select an accent color, try repeating it somewhere else in your outfit. For example, when wearing a black suit with a red blouse, you might want to wear a pair of red earrings or a red and black pocket-handkerchief.

Summary

Make certain you are sending the message that you want others to receive. It is true that many people make judgments about your competence, background, education, abilities, and confidence based on the way you look, dress, and carry yourself. It is to your advantage to try to bring out your best.

Actor Cary Grant was once asked by a reporter, "Have you always been so confident and sure of yourself?" Cary Grant replied, "When I decided what I wanted to do with my life, I thought about the person I wanted to become and gradually I became that person."

Think about the person you want to become and the steps you can take to help you reach your goals. Part of your success will be achieved by projecting a positive self-image through your appearance.

Appearance Checklist

Check the items you might want to change and then take this list to your closet, your hairdresser, and your favorite shops. Assemble a few outfits that would be suitable for making a presentation, using this checklist as a guide.

Accessories

- ☐ Wear jewelry that is simple and not distracting.
- ☐ Be consistent with your jewelry.
- ☐ Avoid jewelry that can be noisy and distracting.
- ☐ Wear large earrings.
- ☐ Anchor scarves and pocket-handkerchiefs.
- ☐ Wear a belt for a finished look.
- ☐ Carry a quality leather handbag or attaché case that is not too large.
- ☐ Wear conservative ties.
- ☐ Wear quality, conservative socks or stockings.

Shoes

- ☐ Wear quality shoes.
- ☐ Select classic shoe styles over fads.
- ☐ Wear shoes as dark or darker than your hemline.
- ☐ Match shoe clips to the same gold or silver tone of your jewelry.
- ☐ Keep your shoes polished and in good repair.

Clothing

- ☐ Select an appropriate garment for the occasion.
- ☐ Dress as well as the best-dressed person at the occasion.
- ☐ Wear a jacket for power and authority.
- ☐ Buy quality fabrics.
- ☐ Buy classic pieces.
- ☐ Select solid-colored garments.
- ☐ Wear accent colors that enhance your appearance.
- ☐ Select styles appropriate for your age.
- ☐ Have clothes tailored for a good fit.
- ☐ Wear your hemline at the knee or below.
- ☐ Power dress appropriately; express your own style.

Cosmetics

☐ Use makeup moderately. Go to a makeup artist or attend a class on color, products, and application.

☐ Have your nails manicured; avoid excessive lengths and bright nail polish.

☐ Do not drum your nails on a table or lectern; it's distracting.

Hair

☐ Wear a hairstyle that is neat and not trendy. For a business look, hair at shoulder length or above is best.

☐ Avoid a hairstyle that falls forward into your face or long bangs.

Color

☐ Wear colors that make you feel good and ones that people compliment you for wearing. Have your colors analyzed by a color expert.

☐ Wear darker colors for a more powerful look.

☐ Choose bright solid colors for a television or media appearance.

☐ Match a bright-colored blouse with a contrasting suit.

☐ Select a color that supports the message you want to convey.

Color	Tone
Teal	Open communication
Bright yellow	Learning
Red	Energy
Orange	Agitation
Pink or blue	Calming, trusting

☐ Repeat an accent color somewhere else in your outfit.

Section Two

Preparing to Present

This section takes you into the arena where you deliver your message. Although this section and the next discuss the activities performed by polished speakers, the ideas and skills you'll learn can be applied to a variety of speaking situations. Whatever the purpose of your presentation, you can increase your effectiveness if you take the time to plan, prepare, and practice. These steps combined with the essential communication skills in Section One will help you present with flair.

6

Organizing Your Presentation

If you don't know where you're going, you could wind up some place else.

Yogi Berra

As soon as you know you are going to be giving a presentation, consider the overall purpose, what you want to accomplish, and to whom you are speaking. Effective communication involves more than an exchange of ideas; it requires planning and organization. Like glaciers, the bulk of a powerful presentation is hidden to the audience. The unseen planning, preparation, and practice enable the polished speaker to deliver his or her message with apparent ease.

This chapter includes several work sheets to help you organize your ideas more quickly and easily. You can also adapt these guide sheets to suit your particular purposes. Use whatever works best for you.

Preparing to Speak

Your presentation begins the moment you agree to speak. If you immediately start preparing, you'll maximize your time and energy.

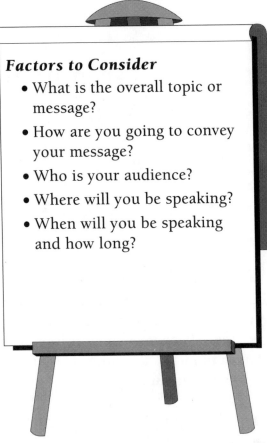

Factors to Consider
- What is the overall topic or message?
- How are you going to convey your message?
- Who is your audience?
- Where will you be speaking?
- When will you be speaking and how long?

What is the overall topic or message?

Begin making notes of any ideas that come to you. Writer Robert Benchley commented, "It seems to me that the most difficult part of building a bridge would be the start." Writing is no different. You have to brainstorm. Put some ideas on paper about your possible themes and then decide on one main point or message. Your objective is to be able to define this overall message in one sentence. For example, "In my presentation, I will discuss the impact of illiteracy on our society." Your audience needs a clear picture of your message.

Not too long ago, I was talking with a man at a party who told me that he had written a book—a very long book that required years of his time. He complained that he was unable to get the book published after innumerable attempts. I asked him to tell me the main idea, or theme, of the book. He began to tell me, and after five minutes my eyes were beginning to glaze. I had no idea what he was talking about. If he couldn't tell me the main idea of his book, how could publishers or readers understand his thinking? Having something to say and saying it in a way that readers or listeners will understand is critical to any presentation, book, speech, or report.

One effective method for stimulating ideas and thoughts on your topic is called mind-mapping, or pattern notes. This is a creative technique for individual brainstorming. Although an outline is useful for arranging information, it tends to draw on a limited part of our powerful mental system. Recent brain research shows that the brain processes thoughts and ideas in interrelated networks. Mind-mapping enables the brain to work more naturally and completely. Try this technique for stimulating ideas. The next method, the more traditional outline, will help you take your ideas and logically organize them.

Brainstorming With a Mind-Map

1. Using a plain sheet of paper, write the purpose of your presentation in the center of the page.
2. Explore the topic by writing down all the ideas and thoughts you have on the subject. Use lines branching from the main theme.

3. Allow your ideas to flow freely. Don't worry about where to place your ideas; simply branch out from the center idea. Connect related ideas to their main branch, as shown in the illustration.

4. Once you have recorded your thoughts, look at the entire map and consider their relationships. As you examine the ideas, look for priorities and logical sequences. (You might want to put it aside for awhile and examine it later. Another perspective can appear that will generate new ideas.)

5. To organize related ideas, try the next technique of using an outline. Work Sheet 7 gives another approach to organizing your thoughts once you've identified the general content.

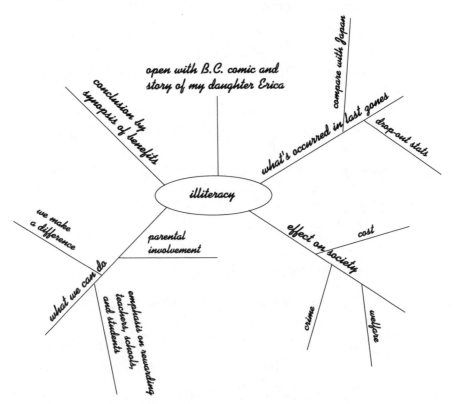

Write down any ideas that come to you. Save articles, quotations, and anecdotes that may be appropriate. It is better to have too much material than not enough. You can always eliminate material that doesn't work or save material for a future speech. Think about a snazzy title that captures the essence of your talk.

How are you going to convey your message?

1. *Introduction:* Create an opening that will grab the audience's attention—a quotation, an anecdote, or a brief humorous story that relates to the topic. You need to gain the attention of your audience within the critical first two minutes.

Avoid opening any presentation with "Good morning afternoon or evening," or a sentence such as "It's a pleasure to be here." Sometimes presenters begin with "Good morning" and then wait for the audience to answer back, but the response doesn't come because the audience has heard the same thing from the three previous speakers. The usual greetings are so overdone that people literally tune them out. Instead, start out with the unexpected. Open your talk with an unusual or funny quotation, an amusing story, or a fascinating statistic.

2. *Body:* After you've grabbed the audience's attention, begin the classic structure of a speech.

    a. Tell them what you're going to tell them.

    b. Tell them.

    c. Then, tell them what you told them.

Many people are afraid of sounding redundant, but it is possible to say the same thing in many different ways. The average person needs to hear something seven to fifteen times before he or she will remember the message.

Let the audience know what you're going to talk about and why it concerns *them.* The audience is always asking,

"What's in it for me?" Make it clear to the audience that you care about them and why it is to their advantage to listen.

Use examples, illustrations, statistics, anecdotes, or stories to back up each point that you make in your speech. Stories about people always help others relate to your message. For example, I might say to an audience, "In some school districts as many as 40-50 percent of students are dropping out, and test scores are also dropping." I can make the statistics and problems more real and understandable by adding illustrations, such as, "In California, some graduating high-school seniors could not identify the Pacific Ocean on a map. While some students did not know if New York was east or west of San Francisco, still others thought that Socrates was an American Indian Chief and that *The Great Gatsby* was a magician." By giving real information to listeners, they can better understand what you are attempting to relate.

3. *Conclusion:* Tie your introductory comments to your conclusion. Leave your audience with a closing thought that either calls them to action or inspires them to do something. Avoid closing with "Thank you."

Work Sheet 7
Organizing Your Presentation

How are you going to convey your message?

After you have your theme in mind, begin a file with separate sheets or cards.

1. Introduction

2. Body of the speech or presentation

Determine your main points. Three usually work best.

a. Point One

b. Point Two

c. Point Three

Embellish with examples, illustrations, anecdotes, statistics, and so on.

3. Conclusion

Here's an example of how I used this format for a speech I gave about illiteracy in America.

I opened with a short joke from a *B.C.* comic strip pertaining to education.

I told the audience that I was going to discuss (1) what has been going on in education during the last twenty years, (2) why illiteracy concerns all of us, and (3) what the future holds for education and literacy in America. I related the appalling figures on illiteracy in America, as opposed to Japan where there is almost universal literacy.

I concluded with an inspiring note after saying, "It doesn't matter whether we are reading *B.C.* comic strips at the breakfast table or the classics after dinner, whether we're going to Toastmasters once a week, or adult education at night. We have to be the role models for our children and our peers. Collectively we can reverse the trends of the last twenty years—we have to, because literacy is an issue that concerns all of us. The future successes of this country depend upon it. As Coach Lou Holtz told his players at Notre Dame, 'First we'll be *our* best, then we'll be *the* best.' A more literate America will be an America at its best."

During the closing, I again mentioned the *B.C.* comics. It tied the speech together and let the audience see the logic in my material. Work Sheet 8 can help you organize a talk in this format.

Work Sheet 8
Presentation Outline

Title: (Make it short and snappy.)

Introduction: (Grab the audience's attention.)

Body: (Tell your audience the three main points to be covered. Then tell them.)

1. (Main point. Reinforce with examples, stories, illustrations, statistics.)

2. (Main point. Reinforce with examples, stories, illustrations, statistics.)

3. (Main point. Reinforce with examples, stories, illustrations, statistics.)

Summarize the main points.

Conclusion: (Close and call them to action or leave them inspired.)

Who is your audience?

While preparing your presentation, find out who will be in your audience. Most professional speakers have a prepro-gram questionnaire they complete with the help of the person who has organized the program. Whether or not you are a professional speaker, you will come across as more professional if you pay attention to the details of audience analysis. Work Sheet 9 helps you gather this information.

It is extremely important to know your audience. A given topic must be adapted for the needs and interests of the listeners. No matter how dynamic your talk, it will not be successful if it isn't relevant to the audience's needs. Also, audience information guides the appropriate use of examples, humor, illustrations, and participation.

Another way to obtain information about your audience is to ask well-formed questions. A presenter can involve and compliment his or her audience with well-placed questions. Here are some examples of questions I sometimes pepper throughout my programs:

How many of you absolutely love public speaking?

How many of you have never had a fear of public speaking?

How many of you would like to turn your fear into excitement?

What do you hate about meetings?

Who do you admire for their communication skills?

What are the speaking qualities you most admire?

What would you like to change about your own presentation style?

What did you notice when you watched _____?

What positive or negative qualities did you hear when you listened to the tape-recorded voice?

In what type of speaking situation do you feel most confident?

Ask questions, not for the sake of having something to say, but for the desire to understand. Then, listen to the answers. You will learn the needs, objectives, and wants of your audience. Until you know what the members of your audience want and need to know, you can't provide it. As Zig Ziglar likes to say, "You can get everything in life that you want if you just help enough people get what they want."

Work Sheet 9
Audience Analysis

Audience age range: From _____ to _____

Average age: _____

Educational background:

Job responsibilities:

Number of males: _____ females: _____

Group size: _____

Dress code for this presentation:

Reason/purpose for meeting:

Voluntary or mandatory:

Theme of meeting:

Goal or desired outcome of meeting:

Issues to avoid with this audience:

Special challenges or problems:

Is a question and answer session desirable?

Type of programs presented in the past:

Negative experiences:

Names of previous speakers:

Names of officers or top managers who will be in the audience:

Who will precede my presentation:

Who or what will follow:

Name and title of person who will introduce me:

Time allowed: _____ Starting time: _____
Conclusion time: _____

Who can signal when 5 minutes remain:

Contacts for interview:

Where will you be speaking?

During the preparation stage, you'll need to know what the meeting place will be like and the type of equipment available. Chapter 8 covers different media for supporting and enhancing your presentation. It's important to know what the venue is like before you prepare your visual supports and any activities. For example, you won't want to prepare slides if the lighting is inappropriate, the group is too large, or the equipment isn't available. Also, you want make to sure the room or seating provides sufficient space before you prepare any interactive exercises.

Work Sheet 10 will help you determine the equipment and logistics of the meeting place. You may want to create your own preprogram questionnaire. The more you know, the better prepared you will be. Some presenters mail a preprogram questionnaire to the meeting planner who arranged the program. Others prefer to ask questions in a face-to-face or telephone interview to get the necessary information.

Work Sheet 10
Equipment and Logistics

Room set-up: U-shape _____ Rounds _____ Classroom_____
Theater _____ Other _____

What is the color scheme of the meeting room?

What type of lighting?

Is a lectern available?   What type?   How high?

Will I be speaking from a raised platform or podium? How high?

Is audiovisual equipment available?

Flip chart _____ Overhead projector _____
VCR/TV monitor _____ Slide projector _____
Computer _____ Teleprompter _____

Is a microphone available? Stationary _____ Lavaliere _____
Hand-held _____

Is any other equipment needed?

Is it okay to have the audience complete evaluation forms?

Is it okay to distribute marketing materials or sell products?

When will you be speaking and how long?

Knowing when you are to speak is important to first determine if you have sufficient time to prepare. You also need to know if the time allowed is sufficient to address the issue. Time parameters also guide you in selecting the number of examples and the details for elaboration. In a *SPEAKOUT* article, a publication of the National Speakers Association, 100 percent of the people polled reported that they disliked speakers going overtime.

Summary

Strong organization helps an audience understand and follow your thoughts. Remember, it is always the speaker's responsibility to make the material easy to comprehend. It has been said that the true sign of genius is to take the complicated and make it simple. That is what good organization will do for you and your audience.

Up to 90 percent of any presentation is in the preparation. With an abundance of information you will feel more confident, better prepared, and better able to customize the material to suit the audience, all of which makes a more successful session.

Checklist

This checklist gives the key steps in organizing your presentation. This, along with the chapter work sheets, provide handy tools for helping you prepare to dazzle your listeners.

Determine the overall topic or message.

- Make notes of any ideas that come to you.
- Brainstorm ideas on paper about possible themes. Then select one main point or message.
- Define your overall message in one sentence.

Organize your message, using Work Sheet 8, Presentation Outline.

- Write down any ideas that come to you.
- Save articles, quotations, and anecdotes that may be appropriate.
- Think about a snazzy title that captures the essence of your talk.
- Identify your audience, using Work Sheet 9, Audience Analysis.

Determine where you will be speaking, using Work Sheet 10, Equipment and Logistics.

Find out when you will be speaking and for how long.

- Determine if you have sufficient time to prepare.
- Determine if the time allowed is sufficient to address the issue.
- Use the time parameters to select activities and amount of detail.

7

Shaping Your Presentation With Humor

Laughter is a tranquilizer with no side effects.
– Arnold Glasow

ottie Walters, author of *Speak and Grow Rich*, advises speakers to "start their speeches with a laugh and end with a tear." Humor early in your presentation will captivate an audience and gain their attention when you need it most. Generally an audience decides within two minutes whether or not they want to listen to you. Appropriate humor is the best attention grabber you can use.

Whenever you present your ideas to a group, you are building a bridge between your experiences and theirs. Along with your carefully organized ideas, you'll want to add humor to support the bridge. Now that you have a rough outline of your presentation, it's time to shape and polish it so that you really shine. This chapter gives some tips for using humor and anecdotes to carry and enhance your message. The next chapter looks at using illustrations and handouts to enrich and enliven your talk.

Using Humor

If you can laugh with a client, you'll do business with that client. In his book *Using Humor for Effective Business Speaking,* comedy writer Gene Perret advises that "Humor can be a powerful ally in getting your message across. It's an ally that many in the business world neglect and ignore. It has a power and it should be used."

Tips for Using Humor
- Use appropriate humor whenever possible.
- Collect appropriate jokes and stories.
- Personalize jokes and stories.
- Deliver humor crisply; avoid apologies, explanations, or excuses.
- Practice humor on the job.

Use appropriate humor whenever possible.

You should use humor in almost every presentation that you give. I can think of only two speeches that I have ever delivered that did not have humor. One speech was about the killing of the late Mayor Moscone of San Francisco; the other was when I spoke for M.A.D.D. and the family of Dr. Anthony Armino in court at the sentencing of the man who killed him in a hit-and-run, drunk driving case. In both presentations, there was nothing funny to say, and humor would have been completely inappropriate.

In other serious presentations, however, I have used humor. For example, when speaking against drunk driving,

I began my talk with a story related to me by former astronaut Wally Schirra. I met Mr. Schirra and his wife on an airport shuttle one morning. We talked for nearly an hour. I asked Mr. Schirra, "Were you frightened the first time you went into space?" He answered, "The first time, I was a whole lot younger and very naive. I remember standing in a row with the seven astronauts and an official from NASA telling us that the odds were fifty-fifty that we wouldn't be coming back. I looked over at the astronaut standing next to me and I thought to myself, 'Poor guy.' " When I tell that story, especially to high school students, I get the point across—with humor—that we never think it's going to be us. It's always the *other* guy.

Collect appropriate jokes and stories.

Gene Perret, author and comedy writer for Bob Hope, Johnny Carson, and Phyllis Diller, recommends that you write down any good jokes that you hear.

Keep a file of jokes and get in the habit of recording and filing jokes and stories when you hear or read them. Then try the jokes out. At first, you might say, "I heard this one on Johnny Carson's show last night..." Then, if the joke doesn't go over, it's Johnny's fault, not yours.

Appropriate humor means material and humor that will not offend others. Never use racial, ethnic, or blatantly sexual material. If your material may offend just one person, it is better not to use it. It's easier to find off-color humor because there is more of it. Many times an audience will laugh at raucous humor out of embarrassment rather than from thinking it's funny. Good, clean material is out there. Be vigilant and you'll find it.

According to Gene Perret, the following seven forms of humor are harmful to a business speaker:

- Slapstick or physical humor
- Gratuitous insults
- Put-down humor
- Sarcasm
- Questionable taste
- Humor that contradicts your personality
- Humor that contradicts your philosophy

Start being more of an observer of humor. When you see something humorous or hear something funny on TV or radio, write it down. Save cartoons or humorous greeting card lines that might be useful in a presentation. The *New Yorker* magazine is also an excellent source of current humor. Cartoons can be made into visual aids by way of overhead transparencies or may simply be interpreted for the audience. I saw a greeting card that showed a career woman on the cover and the caption read, "I'm sick and tired of men accusing women of being wishy-washy." Inside, the punch line stated, "We just wishy they'd do their own washy." That joke would probably go over well with an all-female audience.

Personalize jokes and stories.

Perret also recommends personalizing humor. Instead of saying, "There's a joke about a dog..." say something like, "This morning, in front of my house, I saw a little, black dog running toward my neighbor." Make the joke sound real.

People love to laugh, and people who can laugh at themselves are more confident. Humor should be aimed at yourself. It almost always works better than the Don Rickles type of humor that puts others down.

I like to tell a story about a time when my husband and I were having dinner with another couple. I had met and seen the woman only three times in three years. During dinner, in a hushed tone, she leaned toward me and said, "Guess what's different about me." I hate that question because it really puts me on the spot. I looked her over and guessed, "Your hair? I really like the cut and the way it frames your face." She looked annoyed and said, "No!" and then pointed to the front of her dress. I then asked, "New dress? It's a great color." She looked frustrated and indicated that she was not pointing to the dress but to the cleavage that was revealed by the plunging neckline. "I had surgery!" she then said proudly. I was finally getting the picture. Then she said with some annoyance, "Don't you remember what I looked like before?" I admitted to her that I didn't. She then replied, "Oh, I was about your size!" This story is the absolute truth. I always get a laugh when I tell it, and I don't mind being the brunt of the joke.

People enjoy hearing stories about other people. These personalized glimpses into our lives usually endear a speaker to the audience. People like to relate to speakers and know that they are human. Telling about some embarrassing moments can make a speaker seem more real. I recently spoke with a woman who said that "God has ways of keeping us humble." She went on to tell me that at a church conference one evening, she walked around for twenty to thirty minutes with a paper toilet seat cover stuck to the back of her skirt. We all have our stories to tell.

Another humorous anecdote I sometimes use involves a true story about an incident at the Phoenix Airport. I was in line to board a flight to Boston. In front of me was a young, blonde, attractive woman. Her family (a mother, father, grown sister, and brother) were there to see her off. The good-byes were rather tearful and dramatic. I was wondering to myself if she was moving to Boston to attend graduate school or interview for a corporate job. Finally, her sister gave her one last hug and said, "You just be yourself. Be yourself and they'll love you!" After the family retreated and I was moving along in line with the young woman, my curiosity was aroused and I asked, "Are you going to Boston on business or pleasure?" Without hesitation the woman turned to me and said, "Oh, I'm going to meet my future in-laws for the first time, so I guess it's business!"

That is a true story, word for word. When I relate it to my audiences they laugh with me. True-life stories, comments, quotes, and anecdotes can be some of your best sources. They are yours. You own them, and they come across as original and real. I encourage you to continuously listen for material that you may be able to incorporate into your presentations, from others and from your own experience.

Deliver humor crisply; avoid apologies, explanations, or excuses.

The most successful humor is conveyed using the fewest words possible. Watch and listen for one-liners. Here are a few examples:

- You know you're a modern-day woman when your boyfriend breaks up with you by fax.
- I'm so slow that it takes me two hours to watch *60 Minutes.*
- If you can't say something good about someone, sit right here by me. (Alice Roosevelt Longworth)
- Marriage is a great institution; but I'm not ready for an institution. (Mae West)
- When all else fails, read the instructions.
- Do not take life too seriously. You will never get out of it alive. (Elbert Hubbard)
- I belong to no organized party. I'm a Democrat. (Will Rogers)

- I didn't know that rock stars could sync so low.
  (Regarding Milli Vanilli, a singing duo)

Avoid undermining your humor or jokes by interjecting comments such as, "I'm terrible at telling jokes," or "I hope you haven't heard this one."

One evening while I was attending a book publicist meeting, the guest author/speaker was asked to tell a joke. Unfortunately, she said yes and proceeded to the front of the room while bemoaning the fact that she had consented to telling the joke. She made comments such as "I can't believe I'm doing this! I'm terrible at telling jokes." She then continued to interject comments throughout the joke ("Oh, why I am doing this!" and "Oh, I hope I get the punch line right!"). She took five minutes to tell a one-minute joke. In five minutes she succeeded in frustrating the audience and ruined her credibility as a speaker, an author, and a professional.

It's always best to avoid apologies, explanations, or excuses. Practice telling one-liners, anecdotes, and humorous stories to your family, friends, and audiences and see what works best. If a joke doesn't get a laugh, it's okay to give people permission to laugh. You might say, "Well, at least my mom thought that was pretty funny!" Johnny Carson sometimes got his biggest laughs when the joke bombed and he simply looked at the audience or at Ed McMahon and then blamed his writers. One evening Johnny said, "I come from such a small town," and the audience shouted, "How small is it?" Johnny finished the joke with, "It's so small that we had to put mirrors up at the end of Main Street to make it look bigger." The audience then took great delight in moaning at the joke. Even when the joke got such a reaction, Johnny dealt with it effectively and ultimately made the audience's reaction work for him.

Practice humor on the job.

Overall, the evidence is strong that both individual and group productivity, plus employee health, improve when humor is part of the work situation. Here are some ideas for tapping this priceless resource:

1. Designate a humor bulletin board. After outlining common-sense standards, encourage employees to contribute cartoons, jokes, funny articles, and so on.
2. Incorporate a little humor in your memos. They will get more attention
3. Use humor to reduce stress and conflict.
4. Communicate that humor is allowed in the workplace. Set an example by using it appropriately yourself.

Summary

Use humor whenever possible. Collect appropriate jokes and stories from others and from your own experience. Personalize others' jokes and stories to make them more real to your audience. Deliver your humor crisply and avoid staging disappointment with apologies, explanations, or excuses. When using humor, allow the audience time to laugh. Wait until the laughter peaks and then, when the reaction starts to diminish, begin speaking again. Let others enjoy the moment, and let them absorb the humor before you move on.

Let humor help you make a memorable, positive impact on your audience.

Checklist

Once you've brainstormed and outlined your presentation, use these ideas to polish your presentation with humor.

☐ Use appropriate humor whenever possible.

☐ Collect appropriate jokes and stories; create a file.

☐ Personalize jokes and stories.

☐ Deliver humor crisply; avoid apologies, explanations, or excuses.

☐ Practice humor on the job to develop a naturally humorous style.

- Create a bulletin board for funny material.
- Add a comic touch to your memos and company announcements.
- Use humor to defuse stressful situations.
- Value others' sense of humor and lead by example.

8

Enhancing Your Presentation With Visuals

The medium is the message.
Marshall McLuhan

Research indicates that a speaker can improve an audience's perception of his or her presentation with well-designed visuals. Since most people are visual learners (we remember only 10 percent of what we hear and over 50 percent of what we see *and* hear), you can help an audience retain information with visual aids.

The previous chapter gave some tips for shaping your message with humor and anecdotes. This chapter looks at the use of visuals and handouts to enrich your talk.

Creating Effective Visuals

Visual aids enhance the memory of any presentation by up to 50 percent. Keep in mind that you are your most important visual aid, so you want to make certain that your image is consistent with your message.

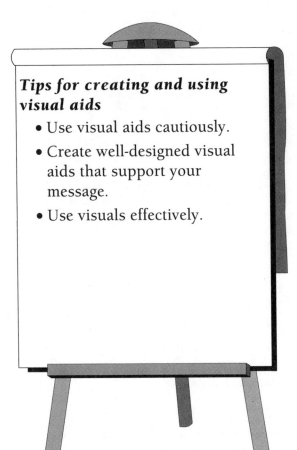

Use visual aids cautiously.

A professional speaker once came on stage with an outrageous outfit, wild looking hair, and lots of plastic jewelry. The audience broke into laughter as soon as she appeared. Her opening comment was, "I'm here to talk about visual aids, and I thought that by dressing like this I would aid you in remembering me!"

Visual aids can be very useful, but they must be used cautiously. If the aid does not enhance the presentation and make for clearer understanding, do not use it. People become fascinated with anything that you hold, put on a screen, or hand out. Some speakers hold onto pens, notes, papers, books, and a variety of other crutches. The audience begins to watch what the speaker is holding and no longer listens to the words being spoken. It is vital that visual aids clarify and add to your presentation, rather than distract.

Create well-designed visual aids that support your message.

Simple, well-designed visuals that support your message are more effective than glitzy visuals that compete with your message. Use the most appropriate and convenient tool to convey your message. It may be flip charts, slides, overhead transparencies, or videotape. Whatever medium you choose, keep it simple and easy to read

Use simple images. Visuals are especially helpful when discussing numbers or statistics. For example, percentages can be made more easily understandable by creating a colorful pie graph rather than by listing a series of numbers. Most people appreciate colorful graphs that can be easily read and absorbed.

Use readable lettering. If you are using a flip chart, the size of the lettering should be

1-inch letters for 30 feet or less

2-inch letters for more than 30 feet

3-inch letters for over 50 feet

You should be able to read the print on slides by simply holding the slide up to a light. If you can read the print, the type size is large enough for the projected image. Your visuals must be visible and readable by all of the audience. People will be upset, frustrated, and resentful if they are unable to see and share in the material that you are presenting.

Limit your points. When listing information on a slide or overhead transparency, limit the amount of information. Writing no more than six points generally works best. (Six items on any one visual is the absolute maximum. Think of billboard advertising.) Make the points brief—not complete sentences, only phrases or main points.

Make notes. If you want to write reminder notes for only you to see, write in pencil on the margins of the flip chart, or write your main points in pencil and simply write over the pencil with colored markers during your presentation. For overhead transparencies, write your notes on the cardboard frame of each transparency. (Frames are available at most office supply stores.) Some presenters place Post-it notes on each transparency with written reminders of key points.

Use bright colors. Using color on visuals adds interest and variety to any presentation. The printing industry has found that color serves to motivate, attract, and sell. One university study showed a 65 percent increase in retention of materials when color was used instead of black and white. Publication-impact studies have revealed a 40 percent increase in readership. Other studies have demonstrated that color boosts the tendency to act. For example, in an ad, color may increase response by 25 percent or more.

Copy paper now comes in dozens of colors and is more pleasing than the standard white paper. Computer-generated slides can be colorful, bright, and bold. Black and white visuals are considered dull. Use watercolor markers (available at most art and office supply stores) for flip charts. They come in a rainbow of colors and do not bleed through the paper the way many permanent markers do. On white boards, use the brightest dry-erase markers you can find—

red, blue, green, purple. Write on the boards with contrasting colors for underlining or for emphasis.

A relatively new product on the market is a dry-erase flip chart called Static Images, made by Dennison. It is available through office supply stores and stationers. Static Images are white plastic sheets that come in flip chart size. The charts have more than thirty sheets that may be torn off and used as needed. The individual sheets stick by way of static to most surfaces (such as glass, wood, walls, most wallpaper, doors, chalkboards). They are useful in adding writing surfaces to any meeting room. Dry-erase markers are used on the Static Images, and the sheets may be erased and used over and over again.

A newer form of transparency is also available for use with overhead projectors. One brand is called CreativColor. The sheets come in a rich, royal blue color and must be used with Pelikan Overhead CreativColor-Markers. The markers are available individually or may be bought in sets with yellow, green, red, orange, and white colors. When the markers are applied to the CreativColor transparencies, the color seems to pop out. Audiences respond positively to the bright colors. With your invisible notes on the border, you can spontaneously create your visuals with ease.

Computer Graphics. Research by 3M Meeting Management Institute, with the University of Minnesota and Wharton School of Business, reported that presenters can improve the audience's perception, comprehension, and retention of their presentations with computer graphics, animation, and graphic transitions.

Computer-generated graphics can be displayed on an overhead projector panel or monitor. A glitzy multimedia presentation won't help an unprepared speaker impress his or her audience, but a good speaker can use animation very effectively to boost audience retention. The study found that "the most effective animations proved to be among the simplest, such as bar charts that grow or text revealed line by line."

Using just transitions (such as wipes or fades) between graphics detracted significantly from the audience's perception and retention. When consistent transitions were combined with animation, audiences responded much better than to transitions alone and slightly better than they did to animation alone.

Use visuals effectively.

Avoid distractions. When using a projector, turn it off if it will be several minutes before you use another slide or transparency. The noise of the projector and the projected image can be a distraction to your audience.

Always face the audience. When using your visuals, avoid turning your back to the audience. For example, if you need to move toward a flip chart or overhead projector, back up while you are speaking. You are usually just a few steps away. When writing on a flip chart, practice standing sideways so that you can continue to look at the audience. When a slide or overhead transparency is on the screen, avoid turning to read the information off the screen. Instead, read the transparency off the projector.

Test the equipment. Practice using the projector before the presentation begins (so be sure to arrive early). Also, check all of your slides to verify that they are in the correct order, not upside down, and that the projected image is in focus. It's advisable to use all-black slides at the beginning and the end of your presentation to avoid the bright, all-white screen. Be sure to have an extra projector bulb with you just in case it's needed. With an overhead projector you can test the focus by placing a coin such as a quarter on the projector surface to check for resolution. When you can see the ridges on the quarter, the projector is focused.

Cue and control information displayed. When you are working with an overhead projector, you may want to reveal information on the transparency as you speak and keep the upcoming material covered by a sheet of paper. You may use a pen, pencil, pick-up stick, and so on as a pointer on an overhead transparency.

Do not use pointers with flip charts or black/white boards. They bring back memories of school for some people. When slides are used for large audiences, some speakers like to use a laser pointer. Laser pointers are expensive, but they can be rented for a small fee from presentation equipment companies.

Hold books, magazines, and pictures for audience viewing. When you hold up an item for the audience to see, hold it still and do not move it until the audience has had time to look. Many speakers will say, "This is a great book!" Then they will proceed to wave the book through the air quickly while the audience tries to focus on the title and author. For example, when showing a book, hold it high enough for all to see. Read the title and the author. Then use the palm of your hand as a shelf underneath the book while your other hand holds the edge of the book without covering the title.

Many excellent presentation skills and tips may be learned from some of the free materials made available by corporations such as Polaroid, Hewlett-Packard, and 3M. Software applications, such as Power Point for Apple computers and Freelance for DOS-based machines, provide ready-to-use formats for producing professional looking visuals. You will find some additional sources in the Resources section.

Creating Effective Handouts

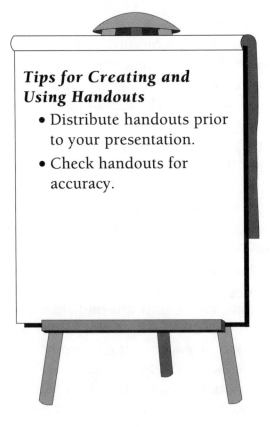

Tips for Creating and Using Handouts

- Distribute handouts prior to your presentation.
- Check handouts for accuracy.

Distribute handouts prior to your presentation.

Presentation handouts help your audience to retain more information about your topic and encourage your audience to remember you.

Any handout that you use in your program should be already be in place when your audience enters, or distributed prior to your opening remarks. If you distribute handouts during your presentation, participants will want to read and look over the materials. They will not be paying attention to you. If it is necessary to give the handouts to your audience during the meeting, wait until everyone has the material and you have the audience's attention again before you speak. You may also distribute handouts after your presentation to serve as a synopsis or reminder of your program.

Check handouts for accuracy.

Check and recheck for spelling errors, inaccuracies, and incomplete information. I recently received a mailing for a seminar that had no return address for reservations. Check for the obvious and not-so-obvious. Ask a friend to help you with proofreading. Be sure to put your name on the handout. (If you are quoting from someone else's work, be certain to give credit to the author.)

Some presenters like to hand out a copy of their slides or transparencies, which makes it easy for listeners to follow and take notes on the presentation. Here are some tips for preparing handouts.

- Make sure the content is accurate and grammatically correct.
- Write in an active, direct, friendly style.
- Use a consistent format for multiple pages.

- Clearly label diagrams and charts.
- Provide sufficient white space for note taking.

Summary

Visuals and handouts can significantly increase the impact of your message. They reinforce and magnify your presentation. All handouts, flyers, and materials should be professional looking so that they reflect your high standard of excellence.

Remember, visual aids will enhance the memory of any presentation by up to 50 percent. Enhance the perception of your presentation and the retention of the audience by using visual supports.

Checklist

Once you've organized your presentation, use these ideas to polish your presentation with visual aids and supplementary materials. Remember, visual supports enhance your presentation up to 50 percent.

Create effective visual aids.

☐ As the most important visual, make certain that your image does not detract from your message [see Chapter 5].

☐ Avoid distracting visuals, such as pens, notes, papers, books, and other crutches.

☐ Use simple images and bright colors.

☐ Use readable lettering that is visible by the entire audience.

☐ Use phrases or main points, not complete sentences; do not exceed six points.

☐ Make notes on the margins of flip charts, on the frame of transparencies, or on Post-it notes on transparencies.

Use visuals effectively.

☐ Test the equipment. Verify that visuals are right side up and the projected image is in focus. Carry an extra projector bulb.

☐ Turn off the projector when pausing significantly between visuals.

☐ Always face your audience.

☐ Cue and control information displayed. Avoid pointers.

☐ Hold any print materials [book, magazine, picture] still until the audience has had time to look.

Create professional handouts.

☐ Check and recheck for accurate and complete information.

☐ Make sure content is grammatically correct.

☐ Write in an active, direct, friendly style.

☐ Use a consistent format for multiple pages.

☐ Clearly label diagrams and charts.

☐ Provide sufficient white space for note taking.

☐ Distribute handouts prior to your opening remarks.

9

Rehearsing
Your
Presentation

Abraham Lincoln wrote the Gettysburg Address on the back of an
envelope while travelling from Washington to Gettysburg.
Louis Untermeyer

Preparation and practice are crucial to dynamic and powerful speaking. Actress Barbara Stanwyck was once asked what made her a success in her profession. She said, "Just two things I recommend that people do. Start on time and know your lines." Similar to acting, dress rehearsals help speakers become familiar with their role and anticipate the actions they'll take and the mistakes they'll avoid.

This chapter integrates the essential communication skills from Section One with the speech material you've prepared in Section Two. Rehearsing your presentation will give you the confidence that comes from having done something before.

Practice for Excellence

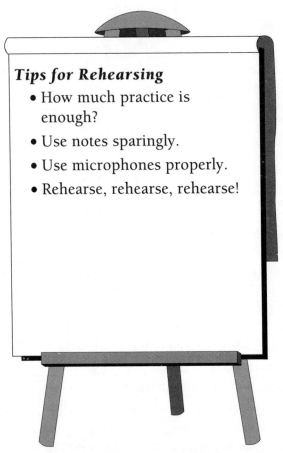

Tips for Rehearsing
- How much practice is enough?
- Use notes sparingly.
- Use microphones properly.
- Rehearse, rehearse, rehearse!

How much practice is enough?

Woodrow Wilson was once asked how long he took to prepare a ten-minute speech. He said, "Two weeks."

"How long for an hour speech?"

"One week."

"How long for a two-hour speech?"

"I am ready now," Wilson replied.

For most people, the shorter the speech, the more preparation that is required. For a five- to seven-minute speech, every word has to count. You should not have any nonessential or *filler* words. Thomas Jefferson said, "Never use two words when one will do."

Successful speakers learn how to prepare succinct, content-rich presentations. Winston Churchill was asked how much he charged to make a speech. He replied, "$2,000." The inquirer responded with, "That's a lot. We only wanted you to talk for ten minutes." Churchill said, "In that case, it will cost $4,000."

I once asked Jeff Young, a past winner of the Toastmasters International World Championship of Public Speaking, how many times he had practiced for the competition. He answered without hesitation, "At least two hundred times." It is necessary to practice over and over again when you're going up against some of the best speakers in the world. For most presentations a minimum of seven full rehearsals is adequate. That may sound like a lot of practice, but the time devoted to rehearsal will make a difference in your level of confidence.

For a lengthy presentation (several hours or an all-day program), it is almost impossible to practice six times. However, you can practice your introductory comments as well as your conclusion and your main points. Know these portions of your program inside out. Know your main points, examples, anecdotes, illustrations, and stories.

Use notes sparingly.

You don't need to write your speech word for word unless it is imperative that the wording be exact (as a diplomatic or press release might require). Instead, write in outline or mind-map format. You should write out any quotation, information, and statistics that need to be accurate; but the main text of your speech should sound conversational, not formal. People can hear the difference between a written text and a more natural conversational tone.

Never read your speech to the audience. When using notes, familiarize yourself with the material in order to have eye contact with the audience at least 75 percent of the time—90 percent is ideal. People don't like to have a speech read to them.

If you must use notes, use 3" x 5" or 5" x 7" cards. Note cards are smaller and make less noise than standard notebook paper. Don't take your entire speech with you to the lectern. Write an outline with bullet points as reminders. Write in large, bold print so that you will be able to read the material easily. (When we are nervous, it is very difficult to focus our eyes on small print.)

When you speak from the heart, your message is conveyed in shorter phrases, is not flowery, and does not have an excess of fancy words. To sound more natural, use contractions such as can't, didn't, won't, instead of cannot, did not, and will not. When we speak in a manner that's too exact, we come across sounding artificial. This does not mean that you can use sloppy grammar. For example, don't leave the beginnings or endings off words such as tell 'em or comin', goin', or doin'. (Unfortunately, this is a common occurrence.) Speak the same way you would with a friend. Be sincere and people will relate to your message.

Use microphones properly.

How strong is your voice? How large is your group? By using a microphone properly, you can use a much broader range of volume variety and captivate a large audience. If you plan to use a microphone, arrive at least one hour before the event convenes so that you can practice using it.

1. Find out, in advance, what type of microphone you will be using (for example standing, attached to the lectern, hand-held, or lavaliere).
2. When you arrive, test the equipment for the sound level and any interference or feedback.
3. If you want to move into the audience, see how much cord length you will have with a hand-held or lavaliere microphone.
4. Check for the appropriate positioning of a lavaliere (lapel) microphone and practice placing it on your jacket and clipping the power pack to the back of your waistband. (Hide as much of the cord as possible.)

5. If you are working with a stationary or hand-held microphone, hold it at a 45-degree angle and several inches away from your mouth so that you can avoid making popping sounds.

Rehearse, rehearse, rehearse.

Practice speaking in front of a mirror and use a tape recorder at the same time. A video camera is even better. As you practice, assess your use of vocal variety, body language, eye contact, and your overall appearance.

If you have a supportive friend who is willing to listen, rehearse with a live audience. You may also want a professional trainer or coach to help you prepare for an especially important presentation. Use the Rehearsal Work Sheet to guide your rehearsals, to assess yourself, or to get feedback from another.

You might find it easier to practice by focusing on only one or two skills each time. For example:

1. The first rehearsal might focus on simply presenting the content to get a general sense of the time and flow of ideas, using notes.

2. The second rehearsal might focus on your voice and adding emphasis, enthusiasm, drama, and entertainment. Consider your use of language, vocal projection, variety, pace, and pitch.

   If you will be using a microphone, practice with a prop so that you can rehearse your positioning and movements. Allow time ahead of the actual presentation to test the equipment and placement.

3. During the third rehearsal, add gestures to portray and reinforce your message. Watch to see if your body language is communicating the same message as your words. Consider your use of physical space, your posture and position, your moves, and how you use your hands.

Practice gestures that reinforce what you are saying without looking mechanical or too rehearsed. Keep in mind that the larger the audience, the larger your gestures must be. At first it will feel unnatural to fully extend your arm—or reach up high—to gesture, but think of how much more effective it will be if you are speaking to a large audience. The people at the back of the room will appreciate your movements.

I observed a speaker who stood behind a lectern while addressing more than 300 people for one hour. She never moved away from the lectern and gestured only occasionally by moving her hands slightly. To the people at the back of the auditorium she appeared to be just a talking head. In order to appear energetic and enthusiastic about your topic, you need to gesture and have your body language in sync with your message.

4. During the fourth rehearsal, look at your use of eye contact. Remember, eye contact helps you gain control. Establish contact with the entire audience and use your eyes to add emphasis, focus, and rapport.

5. During the fifth rehearsal, look at the image you are projecting. Do you appear nervous? Remember the techniques in Chapter 1, the ABCs of managing nerves. Think about your desired outcome as if it already exists. Include affirmations on your notes, outline, and visuals. Remember to breathe deeply and slowly. Practice composing yourself during your rehearsals, and it will seem more natural to do so at your presentation.

6. During the sixth rehearsal, consider your use of humor. Use it often, use it appropriately, and make it personal. Your delivery should be natural and entertaining.

7. During the seventh rehearsal, consider your use of supporting materials. Rehearse with your visual aids so that you feel comfortable using them. Keep your visuals in the order of their use in your program. Make sure your visuals are simple, readable, and colorful. Check out the equipment beforehand so you know how to use it. If you use handouts, remember that they reflect and advertise you; make sure they appear professional.

Use Work Sheet 11 as you go through the seven rehearsals for your next presentation.

Work Sheet 11
Rehearsal Work Sheet

As you rehearse, note areas you want to improve or change. If you rehearse several times, you might focus on one point at a time and refine each point during the rehearsal of the next point. Put these points in whatever sequence you prefer. It's easier to evaluate yourself if you videotape your rehearsals.

1. General time and flow of ideas, using notes

☐ Conversational, logical flow
☐ Ease and legibility of notes
☐ Sufficient amount of information, examples

2. Vocal qualities (refer to Chapter 2)

☐ Appropriate language
☐ No filler words
☐ Varied vocabulary
☐ Voice projection
☐ Vocal variety
☐ Comfortable, stimulating pace

3. Gestures (refer to Chapter 3)

- ☐ Use of physical space
- ☐ Erect posture and chin up
- ☐ Positioned evenly on both feet
- ☐ Deliberate moves
- ☐ Hands relaxed at sides
- ☐ No distracting items
- ☐ Gestures create congruence with message

4. Eye contact (refer to Chapter 3)

- ☐ Eye contact established with audience to gain control
- ☐ Every section of the audience looked at
- ☐ Eye contact held several seconds before moving on

5. Image Projection (refer to Chapters 1 and 4)

- ☐ Appear confident, calm, composed
- ☐ Professional image: garments, accessories, shoes, face, hands, hair

6. Humor (refer to Chapter 7)

- ☐ Used whenever possible
- ☐ Appropriate humor
- ☐ Personalized humor
- ☐ Delivered crisply; no apologies, explanations, or excuses

7. Supporting Materials (refer to Chapter 8)

- ☐ Enhance presentation
- ☐ Created effectively; simple, readable, and colorful
- ☐ Visuals and equipment used effectively
- ☐ Created professional handouts; accurate, organized, and consistently designed; included business information

Work Sheet 12 is a helpful Presentation Checklist that you can use to be sure you have considered all needs with regard to material, equipment, and facilities. The checklist is followed by some figures that show suggested room setups.

Work Sheet 12
Presentation Checklist

This checklist can be used when planning the items you need to prepare, reserve, or communicate to others.

Materials

☐ Visual aids
☐ Notes
☐ Handouts/workbooks
☐ Games/props
☐ Certificates
☐ Books/tapes for sale or recommendation
☐ Business cards
☐ Biographic sketch/promotion materials
☐ Order forms/price sheet
☐ Cash box/change
☐ Visual markers, pencils, chalk, pens
☐ Color Burst film/markers
☐ Masking tape
☐ Name tag or name tent per participant
☐ Pointer

Equipment reservations

☐ Overhead projector with extra bulb
☐ Video monitor, player, tapes
☐ Slide projector and tray
☐ Projection screen
☐ Audiotape player, tapes
☐ Flip chart and easel
☐ Computer

Solid Square

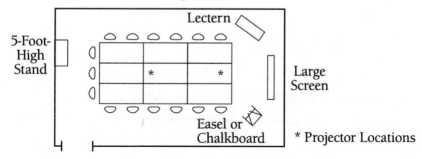

Classroom or Amphitheatre

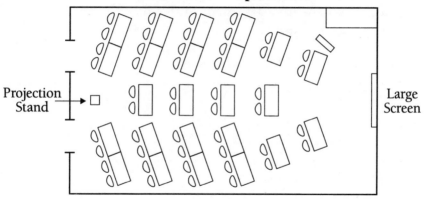

U-Shape/Outside Only

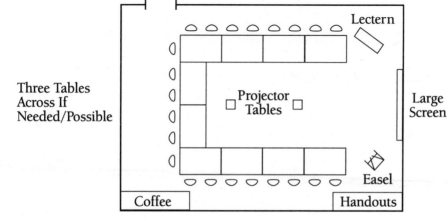

Summary

Rehearsing your presentation at least seven times will give you a boost of confidence.

Practice using notes and microphones effectively. Polish your message with humor. Rehearse with your visual aids so that you feel comfortable using them. Know how long you will devote to each portion of your presentation so that your timing will be correct. Apply your skill in using your voice, gestures, and eye contact to deliver your message. Present yourself calmly, in the appropriate attire.

Practicing ahead of time will give you the edge of professionalism you want to project and will help ensure an excellent presentation.

Section Three

Delivering With Pizazz

The mind is a wonderful thing. It starts working the minute you're born and never stops until you get up to speak in public.

Now that you are using the skills of communicating effectively, you are prepared to speak in a variety of situations. The basic communication skills presented in Section One and the planning process discussed in Section Two apply to any type of speaking situation.

Section Three presents some ideas that will help you deliver your ideas with pizazz. Starting off with effective introductions, using professional speaker etiquette, taking questions from the audience, and managing impromptu speaking situations are special skills that separate the experienced speaker from the neophyte.

10

Speaking Etiquette

I can live a month on a good compliment. After that introduction, I can live forever.

Mark Twain

Mark Twain commented that most introductions were so bad that he refused to let anyone introduce him. Twain would simply walk on stage and introduce himself. Introductions, though, serve an important purpose. If done well, they can enhance your presentation and the reception you receive.

This chapter takes a look at what makes an effective introduction. It also gives some suggestions on how to handle introductions, whether you are being introduced or giving the introduction.

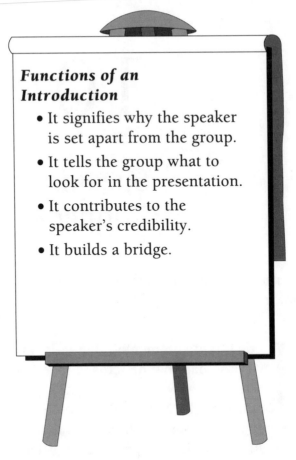

Functions of an Introduction
- It signifies why the speaker is set apart from the group.
- It tells the group what to look for in the presentation.
- It contributes to the speaker's credibility.
- It builds a bridge.

According to Toastmasters International, an introduction has four functions. It is a very important prelude to any presentation. A good introduction sets the mood, tone, pace, and level of enthusiasm that the audience will have for the speaker. It is a responsibility that should be thought out, well prepared, and practiced the same way a speech should be. An introduction should be rehearsed and well-delivered. An outstanding introduction shines a favorable light on the speaker *and* the introducer.

It signifies why the speaker is set apart from the group.

No matter how the well acquainted, well liked, or well known the speaker is to the group, when he speaks, he separates himself from the listeners. He takes on a unique function. He stands and talks while they sit and listen. A good introduction marks the significance of the speaker's transition from being in the group to stepping forth to lead its thinking.

It tells the group what to look for in the presentation.

The listeners will be more perceptive and appreciative if they understand the speaker's goal. Clarifying an idea is quite different from trying to persuade a group to accept a particular point of view. One function of the introduction is to establish the proper mind set so that the group will know what to look for.

It contributes to the speaker's credibility.

Even when the speaker is well-known, the audience might not know what special reason she has for speaking about her chosen topic. They may not be aware of her special experience or expertise concerning the topic. A good introduction contributes to the speaker's credibility by making it clear that she speaks from special preparation, knowledge, or experience.

It builds a bridge.

Before a speaker is introduced, a preceding speech, a round-table discussion, a brief social break, or something else has created the atmosphere, which relates to what has been occurring, not to what will occur. An introduction should build a bridge from the thoughts of the group at the moment to where the speaker wants them to be. An introducer might say, "We have been engaged in serious discussion (or in relaxed conversation, or in listening to an explanation of a new tax law); now I invite your attention to something quite new and different..."

Content of a Good Introduction

Like most speakers, I have experienced some terrible introductions. One time, before I appeared as the scheduled keynote speaker, I gave my prepared introduction to the Master of Ceremonies. Obviously unaccustomed to public speaking, she called the conference to order and said, "I have an introduction about Mary-Ellen Drummond, our speaker. You wouldn't believe all the things she's done and all of the awards she has won. I'll pass this introduction around so that you can read about her." She then called me forward to speak.

Some introducers give such a long-winded introduction that they practically give the speaker's entire presentation. An introducer should avoid delivering information that crosses over into the speaker's territory.

An introduction should not glorify the speaker. The audience might be disappointed. I once heard a speaker say after a more than glowing introduction, "I'm either the wrong speaker or you are the wrong audience."

When you experience a bad introduction, simply go on and ignore what has happened. Sometimes it is difficult to ignore the poor performance of others, and it's tough to say nothing. Once, when I was being introduced, my introducer began talking extensively about another dignitary in the room. He proceeded to lead a round of applause for the other person, and then came back to introducing me. Later, at least a dozen people commented to me about the terrible introduction I was given.

A good introduction showcases the speaker and avoids any personal glorification. Personal experiences should be mentioned only if they relate to the speaker. The speaker should be the consistent theme of the introduction. The audience should know why the speaker has the authority to speak (for example, credentials, background, experience). Create an aura of excitement, interest, and enthusiasm for the speaker without over-billing.

Write your own introduction for any presentation you give to assure that it will be accurate and well written. Mail the introduction to your introducer in advance, or at least have your introduction with you on the day of the performance to give to your introducer.

Consider the elements of a good introduction when writing your own introduction or when organizing an introduction of another speaker.

Elements of a Good Introduction

1. Gains the audience's attention by telling something of interest about the speaker.

2. Tells the audience why the speaker is qualified to speak by giving the speaker's credentials.

3. States the topic of the program and the amount of time for the speaker if the time frame is not obvious or known to the audience.

4. States the title, if the presentation or speech has a title and the speaker wants it known to the group.

5. Asks the audience to join you in welcoming the speaker. Save the speaker's name for last, as it is the signal for applause.

Introductions are usually no more than one minute. The briefer the presentation or speech, the shorter the introduction. The following sample introduction incorporates the elements of a good introduction:

1. Our speaker today claims that fourteen years ago she was terrified of public speaking, just like most Americans. But after seeing herself on videotape, she decided that it was time to conquer her fears.

2. Since that time she has founded several successful Toastmasters clubs and has been named "Toastmaster of the Year" twelve times. Since 1980, she has won more than 75 awards for speaking, training, sales, and leadership. While working for Bristol Myers U.S. Pharmaceutical Division, she was named, "Sales Representative of the Year" for being the number-one representative in the number-one district in the country.

3. For the next thirty minutes, our speaker will demonstrate how to turn your fear of public speaking into excitement.

4. Her program is entitled "Getting Your Butterflies to Fly in Formation."

5. Please join me in giving a warm welcome to our speaker, Mary-Ellen Drummond.

Many people like to say the speaker's name right away when doing an introduction, but it's best to save the name until last in order to create excitement and interest. The speaker's name is the signal for applause. For instance, if I were to introduce entertainer Carly Simon at the Greek Theatre in Los Angeles by saying, "Tonight, we have with us Carly Simon," what would immediately happen? As soon as the entertainer's name was announced, the audience would burst into applause. It is better to create suspense, excitement, and build-up by saying:

"Tonight you are going to hear an incredible performer. We have with us a woman who is not only a premier entertainer, but also a singer, songwriter, and author. She has been performing for more than twenty years and has a long list of hits—from "Anticipation" to the Oscar award-winning soundtrack from the movie *Working Girl*. For the next hour and a half you'll be treated to some of your all-time favorite hits, and you'll hear some of her newest songs. Please join me in giving a rousing welcome to CARLY SIMON!"

One of the all-time great Masters of Ceremonies was Kermit the Frog on Jim Henson's Muppet Show. His introductions of guest performers were excellent. He almost always used the correct format and protocol. A real-life example of excellence can be heard on ABC radio, with nationally syndicated talk-show host Michael Jackson. Jackson is a master at creating an atmosphere of curiosity, interest, and enthusiasm for his guests. Listen carefully to introductions. Determine what creates interest for you and what distracts from the presentation.

Try It Now

Practice developing an introduction right now. Write an introduction for a fictitious speaker or for yourself, using the five elements of a good introduction.

Introducer Etiquette

You don't get a second chance to make a first impression. Whether you are in charge of a program or delivering an introduction, knowing the correct etiquette will give you a greater sense of confidence. First, let's define a few common terms in the speaking arena.

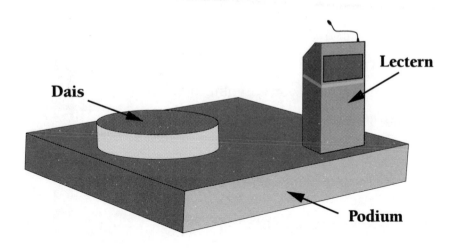

Lectern. A reading desk, a structure built to hold a speaker's notes. It may be a standing, full-lectern or a table-top lectern. It comes from the Latin *legere* (to read). Most people refer to a lectern by calling it a podium, but a podium is something that you stand upon.

Podium. An elevated platform that the speaker stands upon. It comes from the Latin *pod* (foot). Think of the word *podiatrist* as a reminder.

Dais. A raised platform for honored guests.

Presenting a Good Introduction

1. Know what you are going to say in advance.

2. Know where the speaker will be seated.

3. Lead the applause to greet the speaker.

4. As the speaker approaches the lectern, step back.

5. Greet the speaker with a handshake and a smile.

6. After the presentation, return to the lectern and lead the applause to thank the speaker.

7. Present any tokens of appreciation and words of thanks.

8. Stay in the foreground as the speaker steps back.

1. Know what you are going to say in advance.

   If the speaker has not provided an introduction, be sure to interview the speaker and write an appropriate introduction using the five elements of a good introduction.

2. Know where the speaker will be seated.

As the introducer, know exactly where the speaker will be seated in your audience or if the speaker will be seated at the head table.

3. Lead the applause to greet the speaker.

After you complete your introduction, say, "Please join me in giving a warm welcome to _____" and lead the applause. Introducers sometimes forget to lead the applause. The introducer is the leader, and the audience looks to the introducer for guidance and timing.

4. As the speaker approaches the lectern, step back.

Leave room for the speaker to step in front of you. The person relinquishing control of the lectern always steps back and away.

5. Greet the speaker with a handshake and a smile.

When the speaker arrives, greet him or her with a handshake and a smile. Then walk away and be seated quickly.

6. After the presentation, return to the lectern and lead the applause to thank the speaker.

When the speaker is finished, be sure to lead the applause as you approach the lectern to thank the person. Once again shake hands and stand next to the speaker.

7. Present any tokens of appreciation and words of thanks.

Present any certificate, gift, plaque, or token of appreciation and words of thanks regarding the speech just given.

8. Stay in the foreground as the speaker steps back.

After the acknowledgment, the introducer stays in the foreground and the speaker, who is relinquishing control, steps back.

Try It Now

Using the introduction you wrote in the previous Try It Now exercise, practice presenting your introduction, using the eight steps for presenting a good introduction. If possible, videotape your practice for valuable feedback. Identify areas that need improvement.

Speaker Etiquette

As the featured speaker, this is your chance to make a strong first impression. The following guidelines will lead you through the process before and after your presentation.

Responding to an Introduction

1. Anticipate your introduction.

2. Walk quickly to the front of the room.

3. Greet your introducer with a handshake, a smile, and a thank-you.

4. Wait until the audience settles down.

5. Avoid ending your presentation with "thank you."

6. Wait at the lectern or in front of the room until the introducer returns.

1. Anticipate your introduction.

   As you sit in your seat prior to speaking, be ready to go to the front of the room. Have your chair pushed back from the table so that you are ready to get up gracefully and easily.

2. Walk quickly to the front of the room.

   This will create an appearance of excitement and energy on your part. Applause should continue until you reach the lectern or podium. It's uncomfortable for the audience if you walk too slowly and the applause fades before you reach the lectern.

3. Greet your introducer with a handshake, a smile, and a thank-you.

   After you have greeted your introducer with a handshake, a smile, and a thank-you, wait until the person who introduced you has left the lectern and is in his or her chair before you begin. These moments may seem like an eternity, but it is important for you to wait.

4. Wait until the audience settles down.

   Pause, look out at your audience, smile, and wait until everyone has settled down before you say anything. Your timing and demeanor demonstrate confidence.

5. Avoid ending your presentation with "thank you."

   You don't want to end with something ordinary, expected, or uninspiring. Your thanks may be said prior to your close or when you are thanked by the Master of Ceremonies. After a strong conclusion, you might simply address the person in charge of the group and extend your arm in the direction of the person to whom you are returning control of the meeting.

6. Wait at the lectern or in front of the room until the introducer returns.

Again greet the person with a handshake and then step back. The introducer or chairperson may want you to stay in place for a few more moments in order to acknowledge you or present you with a token of appreciation. Be prepared to stay. Don't make a hasty retreat.

Try It Now

Visualize yourself prepared to make a presentation or speech. Practice your response to your introduction, using the six steps for responding to an introduction. If possible, videotape your practice for valuable feedback. Identify areas that need improvement.

Summary

A good introduction sets the audience's mood, tone, pace, and level of enthusiasm for the speaker. Proper speaking etiquette will make you look more polished and professional. Knowing what to do and when to do it will give you a greater sense of self-assurance as a speaker or master of ceremonies.

Take advantage of the opportunity to make a strong first impression. Whether you are in charge of a program, giving a speech, or delivering an introduction, knowing the correct etiquette will give you a greater sense of confidence.

11

Impromptu Speaking

The very difficulty of a problem evokes abilities or talents that otherwise would never emerge to shine.

Most people consider speaking off the cuff to be one of the most difficult assignments. Mark Twain once said, "It takes me three weeks to prepare a good impromptu speech."

The key to successful impromptu speaking is practice. Vince Lombardi said, "Practice doesn't make perfect. Perfect practice makes perfect." Toastmasters International is a good place to practice. They hold Table Topics sessions at meetings where a Table Topics Master calls on members to answer impromptu questions, usually within a one-minute time frame. Questions might be something like this: How do you feel about the issue of Gun Control? What type of movie would you prefer to see—*Gone With the Wind* or *E.T.*? How has Toastmasters helped you in your work?

This chapter presents some tips that will help you speak in impromptu situations, such as when called upon to offer your opinion, when taking unknown questions from an audience, or when being interviewed or prompted with little preparation. With these techniques and practice, you will eventually become more confident and polished about impromptu speaking.

Responding to a Question

Use the tips for impromptu speaking during an interview, personal conversation, meeting, or whenever you've been asked a question. Your answers should take no more than one to one-and-a-half minutes.

Tips for Impromptu Speaking

1. First, get the audience's attention. (You may want to restate the question in your own words.)

2. Tell how you feel, what you think, or give your opinion on the issue or question.

3. Give an example, illustration, or anecdote to help explain your answer.

4. Summarize what you've said.

The following example is in response to the question: How has Toastmasters helped you?

1. That's an excellent question. Toastmasters has helped me in a variety of ways.
2. I know that joining Toastmasters was one of the best things that I ever did for myself.
3. For example, after joining, I found that I was better able to present my ideas during meetings and while working with clients or coworkers. I remember a time, before Toastmasters, when I would have dreaded being called on to answer a question like this. Now, I can honestly say that I look forward to participating.
4. To go from fear to enjoyment of public speaking is the gift that Toastmasters has given me, and it has helped me in more ways than I can count.

Keep your audience in mind when you speak. Take the focus off yourself, and your fear level will decrease. Simply relate your experiences, following the four-step outline for impromptu speaking, and listeners will better understand what you are trying to communicate and will be impressed with your eloquence.

Try It Now

Practice using the tips for impromptu speaking. Practice will make it easier when you later find yourself in an impromptu situation.

Visualize a small or large group in which you are called upon to speak without preparation. For example, you may be attending a luncheon meeting for your organization or for another professional organization and be called upon to share your expertise. You may be in a company meeting, a volunteer group, an interview, or a family setting. Simply imagine a prior experience or a potential future one. You can also practice with a willing friend and use the tips as your format to get feedback for improvement.

Taking Questions from the Audience

There will be times when you must follow up your presentation with a question-and-answer session.

Tips for Question-and-Answer Sessions

- Be enthusiastic.
- Repeat the question.
- Keep your answer brief.
- Don't bluff your way through.
- Give a brief response to an antagonistic question.
- Thank people for their questions and interest.
- Let your audience know that you will answer questions after the presentation.
- Have people in the audience who will ask questions.
- Offer an answer to a question that has not yet been asked.
- Let your body language reinforce that you are eager to answer questions.
- Save a short statement to close your question-and-answer session.
- Be available after your presentation.

Be enthusiastic.

This is an excellent opportunity to share your expertise with the audience.

Repeat the question.

This verifies the question, as well as repeating it for those who didn't hear. Large audiences will especially appreciate the repetition.

Keep your answer brief.

Brevity has power, and most audiences appreciate a succinct presentation. There's an old story about a Yale graduate who was called on to give an impromptu speech at a dinner. He began speaking about his college alma mater, saying that the Y stood for youth, when all might enjoy the benefits of college; the A stood for the appreciation of all of the finer things that college makes possible; the L stood for loyalty from which all sincere endeavor stems. He spent about an hour elaborating on all of this until he ended with E, which he said stood for efficiency of the graduates. Out in the audience, one listener murmured to his neighbor, "Thank God he didn't attend the Massachusetts Institute of Technology."

Don't bluff your way through.

If you do not know the answer, use humor and say, "Boy, this must be Stump the Speaker night! I don't have the answer to that, but I'll try to get that information to you if you'll leave your card with me after the presentation."

Give a brief response to an antagonistic question.

If someone in the audience is antagonistic, you may want to give a brief response and then say, "I'll be happy to discuss this with you further during the break. Does someone have another question?"

Thank people for their questions and interest.

You might say, "That's a great question!" or "Thank you for asking." Make certain that people feel appreciated and encouraged for participating.

Let people know that you will answer questions after your presentation.

Some speakers tell the audience, "I'll be taking questions after my presentation." The audience will then anticipate their opportunity to ask about particular topics.

Have people in the audience who will ask questions.

Speakers sometimes have people in the audience who have been prompted to ask questions if no one spontaneously asks.

Offer an answer to a question that has not yet been asked.

If you have no audience response when you first ask for questions, you might say, "One of the questions I am most often asked is..."

Let your body language reinforce that you are eager to answer questions.

Avoid pointing your index finger at the person asking a question. Instead, use the more inviting palm-up gesture, with your hand and arm extended toward the person you are addressing. When you are speaking to someone, you might place one foot in front of you more than the other. Put your weight on the forward foot and lean slightly forward. This gives the impression that you are reaching out to your audience.

Save a short statement to close your question-and-answer session.

Acknowledge the audience for their participation, then leave them with a brief one-minute inspirational close that you have prepared.

Be available after your presentation.

Be available for comments, questions, and interaction with the audience following your presentation.

 Give 3" x 5" cards to the audience, encouraging them to note any questions that come to mind during the presentation. With very large audiences, you may want several assistants to collect the cards and discern which questions have the broadest appeal to the group.

Try It Now

Practice taking questions from an audience after your presentation using the tips for question-and-answer sessions. Try it a couple of times with a friend or use a video recording.

In the first practice, assume that you don't know the answer to the second or third question. Stay positive and try using some humor.

In the second practice, assume that you don't get any questions at first. When you do, you are met with some hostility.

Dealing With the Media

When you watch television, how many seconds do you, or someone in your household, give a particular program before pressing the remote control to go to the next station? Three seconds? People make instantaneous decisions about what they see on the screen. Remember this when you are asked to appear on TV.

According to the book *In an Average Lifetime*, the average American spends 10,935 hours reading and 117,048 hours watching television. American children spend more of their time in front of the TV than in school. More and more, we are experiencing the power of television.

If you have good communication skills and are actively involved in business or your community, you will probably be asked at some time to appear on a talk show or to be interviewed on radio.

To help you manage an interview situation and deal with contrary points of view, use the following checklist of techniques to practice and apply.

Preparing for the Interview

☐ Read, listen, or watch the medium in which you will be appearing so that you'll have an idea of the style of interviewing done at the particular paper, station, or program.

☐ Determine one main message that you will leave with the audience.

☐ Plan ahead of time what points, facts, and figures you want to make during the interview.

☐ Have examples, anecdotes, or statistics in mind that will back up your point of view. Audiences will remember stories about people more than any other type of example.

☐ Rehearse your statements out loud.

During the Interview

☐ Act as naturally and calmly as possible. Treat the interview as if you were simply having a conversation across your dining room table. A smile will help you come across as calm and relaxed.

☐ Your speaking rate should be about 150+ words per minute to sound lively but not too rushed. Speak as you would one-on-one and not as you would in front of a large audience.

- [ ] Try to make your main points early in the interview. Know what you want to get across and do so succinctly. Most media want ten- to thirty-second sound bites.
- [ ] Be brief when giving answers. Short, powerful statements are best.
- [ ] If you do not understand a question, ask the reporter or interviewer to clarify it.
- [ ] Take the time to pause and think about your answer. You might start off with, "That's an excellent question," and then repeat the question before your reply.
- [ ] If you receive a negative question, try to turn it into a positive response. Avoid repeating a negative question.
- [ ] If your words are distorted in any way, do not hesitate to refute the misrepresentation.
- [ ] Avoid the use of jargon or words that the general public will not understand. If a technical phrase is used, clarify the meaning. It's best not to sound condescending, technical, or academic.
- [ ] If you use notes for a radio interview, use 3" x 5", or 5" x 7", note cards instead of paper. (Microphones will pick up paper noise.)
- [ ] On radio, talk across the microphone and not too close to it. Do not breathe or sigh into it. Soften your b, d, g, p, t, and k sounds.
- [ ] Do not wear any jewelry that moves (for instance, dangling ear-rings), or makes noise (such as charm or bangle bracelets), or that can interfere with the microphones.

Tips for Television

- [ ] Do not hold notes while on television. Some television programs will be willing to put your planned statements on a teleprompter when you deliver an editorial, for example, but not during a talk show.
- [ ] If you are looking into the camera, look toward the one that has a lighted red light on top. That is the *on-air* camera. Be careful to maintain your gaze and avoid wandering. If you are instructed to look at the second camera, the studio floor manager will signal you to the next camera where the red light will be shining.
- [ ] On television, you won't have to worry about the microphones. You will either be wired ahead of time or a boom microphone (suspended from a pole) will pick up your voice.

☐ Avoid tapping your fingers, coughing, rustling, or hitting the microphone. Be careful of what you say. The camera and microphone may be on at any time.

☐ Avoid wearing black-and-white outfits. If possible, watch the program before your appearance and notice the color of the set, chairs, background, and so on. Wear solid colors or colors with striking contrasts (for example, blue and gold, purple and teal). Avoid horizontal stripes. Blue seems to always look good on camera.

☐ It's best to wear a jacket for a professional look. It is also easier to hide microphone wires with a jacket. Conservative attire is generally your safest bet.

☐ Makeup makes a difference. It keeps you from looking washed out by the camera lights. Wear enough makeup to add color without looking overdone. Use natural shades, a flat matte finish, and powder for both men and women to avoid shine. Women should avoid bright eye shadows.

☐ Use meaningful gestures. On television, avoid elaborate gestures or movements that are too sudden or overstated. Unlike platform presentation gestures, keep your body language simple and gestures close to your body. Be sure not to shift your weight back and forth. If you are in a swivel chair, avoid the temptation to swivel.

☐ Avoid looking at the cameras (unless you are reading an editorial). Look at the interviewer who is asking you questions.

☐ Talk with people—not at them—and you'll be a success. Use the interviewer's name at times. If you are on a call-in radio program, repeat the caller's name during your reply. Remember, people don't care how much you know until they know how much you care.

☐ Ask the station producer if it would be possible for you to receive a video or audio cassette copy of your portion of the program. (If not, be sure to arrange for your own taping.)

☐ Thank the interviewer for the opportunity to be a part of the program. Follow up with a thank-you note or letter.

Section Four

Continuous Learning and Improvement

Section One explored some essential skills that can empower and benefit you in any communication exchange. Sections Two and Three focused on preparing an effective presentation and then delivering your message with polish and pizazz. Section Four presents some success tips that distinguish the peak communicators.

Well-organized, rehearsed, enjoyable, and professional presentations will carry you to new levels of communicating in a diversity of situations. One of the crucial elements in achieving greater skill and impact is an attitude and practice of continuous improvement. If you learn from each presentation you do and apply those insights, you will develop your communication skills immeasurably.

12

Evaluations: Giving and Receiving Feedback

You must know your strengths and weaknesses before you can be a real achiever.

The most valuable lessons in life are sometimes learned through mistakes. You should not dislike mistakes. Elbert Hubbard said, "The greatest mistake a man can make is to be afraid to make one." It's true that the person who makes more mistakes (and learns by them) will move ahead in life the fastest.

Babe Ruth is often used as an example of a person who wasn't afraid to try. He held the record for home runs. He also held the record for strikeouts—1,330 times. Everyone who achieves anything of significance in life makes mistakes.

One of the most embarrassing moments of my life was watching a videotape of myself in a business training session. Watching myself make mistake after mistake was terrible, but it was a powerful lesson. I saw what I didn't like and didn't want to be. Up until that moment I had not realized how I came across to others. Videotape doesn't lie. I made up my mind to change. If you learn from your negative experiences, you will not fail.

Giving Effective Feedback

At Toastmasters meetings, all members are asked to give the speaker feedback by filling out evaluation slips, and an individual evaluator completes a specific evaluation form. Effective feedback is arranged using the "sandwich" approach.

Give the speaker some positive feedback right away. Tell what you liked about the speech.

Give one or two suggestions for improvement.

End with a positive message and thanks.

1. Give the speaker some positive feedback right away. Tell what you liked about the speech.
2. Give one or two suggestions for improvement.
3. End with a positive message and thanks.

This formula encourages speakers, helps them to be even better the next time, and leaves egos intact. Giving criticism without suggesting what could be changed and how to change it does not help anyone.

As a speaker, you can build your evaluation forms to provide positive and constructive feedback. You can also use this approach when you evaluate yourself. Use it to become a better listener, evaluator, and audience member. Keep in mind that it takes courage for a novice speaker to get up in front of an audience. Be generous with your encouragement and praise the person for all of the positives that you observed.

Receiving Feedback

Welcome feedback from others about your presentation skills. Keep in mind that you may disagree with another person's perception of you. You have a right to disagree. Listen for comments that you hear several times from several different people. Chances are there is some truth to the message. If you hear an off-the-wall comment, or one from left field, don't spend too much time thinking about it. It is usually from someone who is overly critical. Consider the following advice regarding evaluations: Throw out the very best comment and the very worst and you'll probably find the truth about your performance.

Use evaluation forms whenever you speak. *Listen* to the comments you get on the evaluation forms for consistency. People will tell you what worked and what didn't work, what they liked and didn't like. Be cautious, however, and avoid taking all comments to heart. Some evaluations may reflect the life of a negative person, a highly critical person, or a person who has another agenda. For example, I once did a program for a high-school leadership conference. The students had leadership potential, but many were using their power in a negative way. Rosie Grier was the opening speaker. He was great. He had wonderful examples, stories, and actively involved the audience. On the conference evaluation forms, however, one student rated the opening program a 2 out of 10 and had written *Boring*. Most students rated the program a 9 or 10. In the comment section, the same bored student remarked, "Should have had more donuts and soda."

Many of us remember only the worst evaluations we receive. It's important to remember to look at the whole picture and see how the majority of people responded. The *boring* evaluation may have come from a student who lived in poverty and enjoyed the luxury of soda and donuts, or whose family was experiencing a divorce so the upbeat message was lost.

Learning Through Evaluations

After you present a seminar, workshop, speech, or other presentation, ask the audience to complete an evaluation form regarding your performance. Use the information to prepare your next talk. Here are some frequently asked questions on evaluation forms:

What did you like about the presentation?

What would you like to see changed?

What idea, or exercise, helped you the most?

How did you benefit from this training or program?

How would you rate this presentation on a scale of 1 to 5 (or 1 to 10)?

How would you rate the information on a scale of 1 to 5 (or 1 to 10)?

Any additional comments or suggestions?

May I quote you?

After each presentation, take a few minutes to ask yourself these same questions. Without being excessively critical, recognize and affirm your strengths and consider where you would like to improve. If you collect group evaluations, evaluate yourself first, summarize the group's feedback and compare it with yours, then integrate it into an action plan.

Look for aspects of your presentation that had nothing to do with you, such as room arrangement or audience disruptions, which you would like to better manage next time. Reflect on your options and increase your flexibility as an expert communicator.

As a speaker, welcome feedback, comments, suggestions, and advice as much as you do praise. Of course we all love to hear positive remarks. Norman Vincent Peale once said, "The trouble with most of us is that we would rather be ruined by praise than saved by criticism." We live in a negative world, but it is possible to learn a great deal from the negatives and turn our mistakes into valuable lessons.

In his book *Effective Psychology for Managers*, Mortimer Feinberg wrote, "By making mistakes and risking loss, a man learns things. When John Kennedy lost a bid for the Democratic vice presidential nomination in 1956 to Estes Kefauver, he didn't quit. He said, 'Okay, now we know the mistakes we made; we know what we have to do to win. In 1960 we'll go for the big job.' The rest is history."

If you ever feel really low and rejected after receiving a particularly tough or rude evaluation, consider these famous personalities who have also experienced rejection.

Actor Tom Selleck: "I went on *The Dating Game* a couple of times. I was always Bachelor Number Two, and I was never picked."

Television talk show host Sally Jesse Rafael has been fired 28 times.

Academy Award winner Gene Hackman was voted "Least Likely to Succeed" by his graduating class.

Actor Jack Nicholson: After his first screen test, the director said, "I don't know what we can use you for, but if we ever do need you, we'll need you real bad."

Actress Loni Anderson remembers that in the sixth grade there was a Loni Anderson Hate Club. "It was a terrible feeling being rejected that way."

Luke Perry, television star of *Beverly Hills 90210*: "I took acting classes and tried out for every role in sight. I was rejected 216 times. Exactly. I know, because I kept count."

Actor Dustin Hoffman: "I got up the courage to announce to my family that I was going to be an actor. 'But you can't,' Aunt Pearl said. 'You're not good looking enough.' "

Actress Sigourney Weaver: During her first interview, the interviewer suggested, "Do yourself a favor. Get a sales job at Bloomingdale's."

You never know what people in your audience are experiencing in their personal lives and how those personal experiences may be reflected in their attitude toward you. While it is important to learn from your evaluations, it's also important to disregard comments that do not ring true or those that are simply out in left field. You can listen carefully to others' perceptions, determine what is useful for your own growth, and remain true to your personal goals. As many well-known public figures have said, persistence is what counts.

Acknowledging the Host

William James reminds us that "The deepest principle of human nature is the craving to be appreciated."

After any presentation you give, follow up with a note of appreciation to the person who invited you to speak. Every speech that you give is an opportunity to become your best, and you want to show your appreciation to your host. Unfortunately, very few people take the time to do this. If you do send a note, you will stand out as a professional.

If you have invited a person to speak to a group, follow up the presentation with a note to the speaker. Give special thanks to a speaker who has performed at a reduced fee, or for no fee. It takes hours to prepare for a program, and proper appreciation and acknowledgment should be given.

Small things such as thank-you's and professional follow-up can make a big difference in your career. Always do more than is expected. If you do, you'll make a difference and be a success!

13

Continuing Your Learning

All of us are reaching for the stars, only some of us have our feet stuck in the mud.

Ida Lupino

Nineteenth-century American statesman and philosopher Carl Schurz once said:

> Ideals are like stars.
> You will not succeed in touching them with your hands.
> But the seafaring man who follows the waters follows the stars.
> And, if you choose them as your guides,
> You can reach your destiny.

This chapter mentions just a few of the many excellent speakers who have pursued their ideals. The following resources provide a network of other professionals who can enhance your communication skills. (Note: The Resources section of this book lists addresses and phone numbers of organizations as well as recommended reading for ongoing support.)

Toastmasters International

Joining Toastmasters is one of the best investments you will ever make in yourself. It offers plenty of opportunity for practice so you can make mistakes and *learn* by your mistakes. One Fortune 500 CEO said, "If I'm not making at least 100 mistakes a day, I'm not working hard enough!" You learn only through trial and error, and you will quickly find what works with an audience and what doesn't work.

When Charles F. Luce was Chairman of the Board for Consolidated Edison, he stated, "My five-year membership in Toastmasters was the most valuable club membership that I ever had. It gave me a unique opportunity to learn how to preside at meetings, to speak in public, and to think on my feet—and to do so in a setting where mistakes were not costly."

Toastmasters provides a laboratory for learning where it's safe to make mistakes. And you get plenty of positive feedback for trying. Toastmasters surrounds you with people who are motivated to learn more and to grow. I will be forever grateful to my fellow Toastmasters for the support, encouragement, and inspiration that they have given me.

National Speakers Association

Cavett Robert, professional speaker and author, is one of the founders of the National Speakers Association (NSA). While Toastmasters offers an arena for amateurs to learn, the NSA provides an environment for aspiring and accomplished professionals to continue expanding their abilities.

The NSA has more than 30 chapters in the United States and abroad. With more than 3,100 members, a wide spectrum of individuals are represented. The NSA embraces experienced speakers as well as developing professionals and individuals who serve the speaking profession with products and services such as speakers' agents and bureaus, rally producers, public relations agents, cassette and video producers, and marketing materials specialists.

Local chapter meetings allow for fellowship, informative programs, showcase publications, leadership sessions, speakers' schools, mentor programs, and the opportunity to be published in the local newsletter.

American Society of Training and Development (ASTD)

The ASTD is an international association for people with training and development responsibilities in business, industry, education, government, public service, and other areas of human resource development.

You may be affiliated with a local chapter or with both the local and national ASTD organizations. Members represent a wide cross-section of business from high-technology, tourism, manufacturing, and independent consulting. (Many professional speakers are also professional trainers.)

Throughout the year you may attend local chapter meetings, special educational events, as well as regional conferences and the ASTD's national convention.

Educational Centers

Local community colleges and universities with continuing educational programs are another learning resource.

Personal Development

Get involved with your ongoing education and self-development program. Consider these ideas for becoming more visible and successful:

☐ Visit and join professional organizations where you can learn the latest in innovations or information regarding your field.

☐ Be friendly, professional, and helpful at meetings.

☐ Ask questions of other people and listen well.

☐ Learn from every experience.

☐ Let people know what you do.

☐ Volunteer to be on a committee or support team.

☐ Run for an office or board position within the organization.

☐ Contribute articles to organizations' newsletters to become better known and to establish yourself as an expert.

☐ Say yes when you are invited to be a part of a panel discussion or participate in meetings.

☐ Read material related to your field of expertise for one hour every day.

☐ Listen to educational and motivational cassettes while driving in your car or while going for a recreational walk.

☐ Surround yourself with motivated, positive people who are success oriented and who support your goals.

☐ Visualize yourself as the communicator and person you want to become.

Continue to Set New Goals

Eleanor Roosevelt believed that we can conquer our fear of group speaking by doing it and by continuing to do it until we get a record of successful experiences.

At the beginning of this book, you assessed the areas where you desired improvement, and you set some goals. As you have read this book, you have experimented with ideas, particularly those pertaining to your personal needs and goals.

The majority of successful people set goals and actively review their progress. Review your goal sheet often, continue to speak and evaluate your progress, develop a record of successful experiences, and stretch toward new horizons.

A Final Word

You should always learn, strive to improve, and challenge yourself to be the best you can be. Reach for the stars by setting communication goals that excite you about your future. Take things one step at a time, building on your successes. You can become a communicator with power, polish, and pizazz! Once you make a decision, you can move toward your goals. As Oliver Wendell Holmes said, "The greatest thing in the world is not so much where we are, but in what direction we are moving." May the steps in this book help you move toward becoming your personal best.

**Communicate with Power, Polish, and Pizazz
as you reach for the stars!**

Resources

Organizations

Toastmasters International (World Headquarters)

P. O. Box 9052
Mission Viejo, California 92690
(714) 858-8255, Fax (714) 858-1207

Toastmasters is the largest nonprofit educational organization in the world that is dedicated to better speaking, thinking, listening, and leadership. Toastmasters provides ongoing development programs, conferences, workshops, and contests.

Toastmasters has thousands of chapters in the United States and throughout the world. Many corporations have their own in-house Toastmasters club to help train employees to be better communicators. Usually, clubs meet on a weekly basis with an agenda that features speakers, evaluators, an impromptu speaking session, and a variety of opportunities for learning. Contact Toastmasters International in your area or call the world headquarters for information.

National Speakers Association (NSA)

1500 South Priest Drive
Tempe, Arizona 85281
(602) 968-2552

Some of the benefits of membership include a directory listing in *Who's Who in Professional Speaking*, ten issues of the NSA news publication along with ten *Voices of Experience* audiotapes (top achievers who share their talents and expertise with vital information that members can use to enhance their business and platform skills), networking, local and regional newsletters, professional emphasis groups (PEGs), and recognition awards.

American Society for Training and Development (ASTD)

1630 Duke Street
Box 1443
Alexandria, Virginia 22313
(703) 683-8100

Membership services in the ASTD include new-member orientation, resource library, position referral service, special interest groups, and newsletters. In addition to state-of-the-art knowledge gained from these meetings, socializing and networking with others in the field are exciting aspects of ASTD.

Products

3M Corporate Visual Systems Division- Meeting Management Institute

3M Austic Center, Building A145-5N-01
6801 River Place Boulevard
Austin, Texas 78726-9000
(800) 328-1371

Contact 3M for information and visual supplies. They produce a meeting management newsletter and offer a booklet entitled, "How to Prepare Colorful Overhead Projection Visuals."

CRM Films

2215 Faraday Avenue
Carlsbad, California 92008-7295
(800) 421-0833, Fax (619) 931-5792

A leading producer and provider of corporate training videos, CRM offers a choice selection of powerful communication skills videos. Other topics include total quality management, empowerment, leadership, motivation, and team building. Each video includes a complete leader's guide and may be purchased or rented.

Pfeiffer & Company

8517 Production Avenue
San Diego, California 92121-2280
(619) 578-5900

Pfeiffer & Company (formerly University Associates) is an international publisher of human resource development materials such as reference guides, books, training materials, tapes, video cassettes, trainer's packages, and instruments. Call or write for catalogues.

Recommended Reading

Ailes, Roger. *You Are the Message: Getting What You Want by Being Who You Are.* New York: Doubleday, 1988.

Brandt, Richard C. *Flip Charts: How to Draw Them and How to Use Them.* Richmond, VA: Brandt Management Group, Inc., 1986.

Burley-Allen, Madelyn. *Listening: The Forgotten Skill.* New York: John Wiley & Sons, 1982.

Carnegie, Dale. *The Quick & Easy Way to Effective Speaking.* New York: Pocket Books, 1990.

Cooper, Dr. Morton. *Change Your Voice Change Your Life.* New York: Harper & Row, 1984.

Decker, Bert. *You've Got to Be Believed to Be Heard*. New York: St. Martin's Press, 1991.

Drummond, Mary-Ellen. *Polished Presentations Favorite Quotations/Positive Thoughts for a More Positive Life*. San Diego: Author, 1992.

Gschwandtner, Gerhard. *Non Verbal Selling Power*. New York: Prentice Hall, 1985.

Griffith, Joe. *Speaker's Library of Business Stories, Anecdotes and Humor*. New York: Prentice Hall, 1990.

Leeds, Dorothy. *Power Speak*. New York: Berkley, 1991.

Newstrom, John W. & Edward E. Scannell. *Games Trainers Play, More Games Trainers Play*, and *Still More Games Trainers Play*. New York: McGraw-Hill, 1980-1991.

Perret, Gene & Linda. *Funny Business: Speaker's Treasury of Business Humor for All Occasions*. New York: Prentice Hall, 1990.

Perret, Gene. *Comedy Writing Workbook*. New York: Sterling Publishing Company, 1990.

Richey, David (Ed.). *Meeting Leader's Action Packet*. San Diego, CA: Pfeiffer & Company, 1992.

Sarnoff, Dorothy. *Never Be Nervous Again*. New York: Ivy Books, 1987.

Walters, Dottie and Lillet. *Speak and Grow Rich*. New York: Prentice Hall, 1989.

Yate, Martin. *Knock 'Em Dead with Great Answers to Tough Interview Questions*. Holbrook, MA: Bob Adams Inc. Publishers, 1991.

Index

A

Abdominal breathing, 16, 17

Accent colors, 75
 selecting, 78

Accents
 evaluating, 34-35
 foreign and regional, 34

Accessories
 tips for, 73-74
 using, 75

Accessories checklist, 80

Active listening, 52

Actors, observing, 58, 66

Affirmations, 12-15
 about body language, 63-64
 writing, 15

Affirmative exercises, 24

Affirmative statements, characteristics
 of, 12

Alcohol, avoiding, 22

American Society for Training and Development (ASTD), 175, 180

Anecdotes
 for introductions, 90
 humorous, 106-107
 using, 91

Announcers, studying, 40, 41

Answering machines, leaving messages
 on, 45

Appearance, tips for, 72-78

Appearance checklist, 80-81

Applause, leading, 146, 147

Appreciation, expressing, 170-171

Arms, crossing, 62. See also Body
 language

Articulation, practicing, 39-41

Assess Your Voice work sheet, 26-27

Audience
 analyzing, 94-96
 distractions to, 116
 eye contact with, 68
 feedback from, 69
 focusing on, 22
 getting control of, 68-69
 getting the attention of, 89, 93
 imparting information to, 89-90
 looking at all sections of, 69-70

Audience Analysis work sheet, 96, 99

Audience attitudes, 170

Audience mind set, establishing, 139

Audience questions, handling, 154-158

Authority, conveying, 33. See also Power

B

Benchley, Robert, 86

Bluffing, avoiding, 155

Body language, 55-70
 congruence with message, 61-63
 during question-and-answer
  sessions, 157
 positive versus negative, 60
 rehearsing, 129
 role in communication, 25
 techniques of, 57-66
 voice projection and, 31

Body-language exercises, 63-66

Books, displaying, 118. See also
 Visual aids

Boring voices, 31

Bostonian accent, 34

Brainstorming
 for topics, 86
 using a mind map, 87-88

Breathing, 15-18
 effective, 16-17
 from the diaphragm, 30, 37

Breathing exercises, 17-18, 24

Brevity, in answering questions, 155,
 156

British accents, 34

183